A FRIENDLY GUIDE TO MARK'S GOSPEL

FRANCIS J MOLONEY SDB

Published by
John Garratt Publishing
32 Glenvale Crescent
Mulgrave, Vic. 3170.
Visit www.johngarratt.com.au

Copyright ©2012 Francis J Moloney

All rights reserved. Except as provided by the Australian copyright law, no part of this book may be reproduced in any way without permission in writing from the publisher.

Design and typesetting by Lynne Muir.
Text editing by Ann M Philpott.

Images from www.thinkstockphotos.com.au

Scripture quotations are drawn from the *New Revised Standard Version of the Bible*, copyright ©1989 by the Division of Christian Education of the National Council of the Churches of Christ in the USA. Used by permission. All rights reserved.

ISBN 9781921946202

Cataloguing in Publication information for this title is available from the National Library of Australia at www.nla.gov.au

CONTENTS

Preface 3

When, where and who? 4

Jesus and the disciples 5

Mark's way of telling the story of Jesus 7

The prologue:
Mark 1:1–13 9

The mystery of Jesus:
Mark 1:14 – 8:30 12

    I — Jesus and the leaders of Israel (1:14 – 3:6) 12

    II — Jesus and his new family (3:7 – 6:6a) 15

    III — Jesus and the disciples (6:6b – 8:30) 18

The suffering and vindicated Son of Man:
Christ and Son of God in
Mark 8:31 – 15:47 22

    I — On the way from blindness to sight (8:31 – 10:52) 22

    II — Endings in Jerusalem (11:1 – 13:37) 27

        The end of Israel's cult (11:1–25) 27

        The end of Israel's religious leadership (11:27 – 12:44) 28

        The end of Jerusalem (13:1–23)
        and the end of the world (vv 24–37) 31

The passion of Jesus:
Mark 14:1 – 15:47 33

    Jewish trial: Jesus, the disciples
    and the leaders of Israel (14:1–72) 33

    The Roman trial: Crucifixion, death
    and burial of Jesus (15:1–47) 38

The epilogue:
Mark 16:1–8 42

Preface

Only a year ago, John Garratt Publishing made available my little book *A friendly guide to the New Testament* (Melbourne: John Garratt Publishing, 2010). I am delighted that *A friendly guide to the New Testament* has been so well received, and has helped many people to be gently led into a more informed reading of the books that form part of the literature regarded by all Christians as sacred Scripture. This new 'friendly guide' is an attempt to take that process one step further. Within the covers of *A friendly guide to the New Testament* there are five chapters that remain fundamental for what follows: the emergence of the Gospels (pp 14–15), Jesus of Nazareth (pp 25–27), the synoptic Gospels (pp 29–30), and the two chapters on the Gospel of Mark (pp 31–33, 34–35).

This is an easier book to use. I can now focus upon one single book in the New Testament, the Gospel of Mark. I will be your 'friendly guide' through this challenging story of Jesus. It has long been my concern that, despite the exhortations of the Second Vatican Council and Church leadership since then, many Christians, including most Catholics, are unaware of the authority and power of our biblical tradition. For too many it is unreachable, but for even more, it is not worth the trouble.

This book is based upon my earlier work on the Gospel of Mark, especially *The Gospel of Mark: A commentary* (Peabody, MA: Hendrickson, 2003) and *A year with Mark* (Strathfield: St Paul Publications, 2011). What follows is a further attempt to reach out to all Christians who live under the Word of God, to unlock a powerful story about Jesus, written in rough Greek almost two thousand years ago.

Francis J Moloney, SDB, AM, FAHA
Ascot Vale, Victoria, Australia

WHEN, WHERE AND WHO?

The first readers of the Gospel of Mark encountered a surprising story of Jesus. That was its value. It meant so much to them that they passed it on to successive generations. As we will see, it first appeared about AD 70, shortly after the Letters of Paul, who was executed in AD 64. Mark wrote the first 'Gospel', a *story* of the 'good news' of the ministry, death and resurrection of Jesus. This is the only thing that really matters. But that does not eliminate our curiosity. Something must be said about when this Gospel was written, where it was written, and who wrote it.

In Mark 13, after an introduction (vv 1–4), Jesus speaks to his disciples about the end of Jerusalem (vv 5–23) and the end of the world (vv 24–37). In verses 5 to 23 Jesus speaks of the dangers of false prophets and false Messiahs (vv 5–6, 21–22), and of wars and rumours of wars (vv 7–8, 14–20). He talks about the desolating sacrilege set up in the Temple of Jerusalem (v 14). These details all refer to events that happened before and during the Jewish revolt against Rome that ended with the destruction of Jerusalem in AD 70. The readers of the Gospel of Mark were aware of what was happening or had just happened in Jerusalem. Could this be the end of time, the coming of God's Messiah and judge? Jesus tells his disciples, and Mark tells his readers: 'the good news must first be proclaimed to all nations' (v 10).

There will be an end time (see vv 24–37), but not yet. The Gospel was written around AD 70 to instruct Christians to live bravely, giving witness to Jesus and preaching the Gospel in the in-between time (vv 9–13).

Mark 13 also offers some idea of where it was written and first read and heard. There is an ancient tradition that links this Gospel with Peter and Rome, but that is not likely. The first people who heard this story of Jesus were close enough to know of the war and rumours of wars, and thought that this might be the end. They were probably from northern Palestine or southern Syria. They waited anxiously as the Jewish War drew to its inevitable end, and wondered about the final coming of the Messiah.

Who was 'Mark'? The title 'according to Mark' was not found on the earliest scrolls and books that contained the Gospel. But it was added very early, and was certainly there by the end of the second Christian century. From then on, this story of Jesus has always been known as 'the Gospel according to Mark', even though we are not certain who 'Mark' was. The tradition that associated the Gospel with Peter and Rome also mentions Mark as a 'secretary' or 'interpreter' for Peter. But this does not do justice to the proximity of the first readers and listeners to Israel and Jerusalem.

However, a person named Mark may well have been the author of the Gospel. Mark was a common name, and there is an unfortunate 'Mark' in the early part of the story of Paul in the Acts of the Apostles (see Acts 12:24–25; 15:37–38). Whoever Mark was, he was not an apostle. If the name 'Mark' was attached to the Gospel in the second century, it is more than likely that the scribes who attached that name knew of a tradition of a man named Mark who wrote this Gospel. We cannot be sure, but we will respect the tradition that reaches back to the second century, and always speak of the author as 'Mark', whoever he might have been.

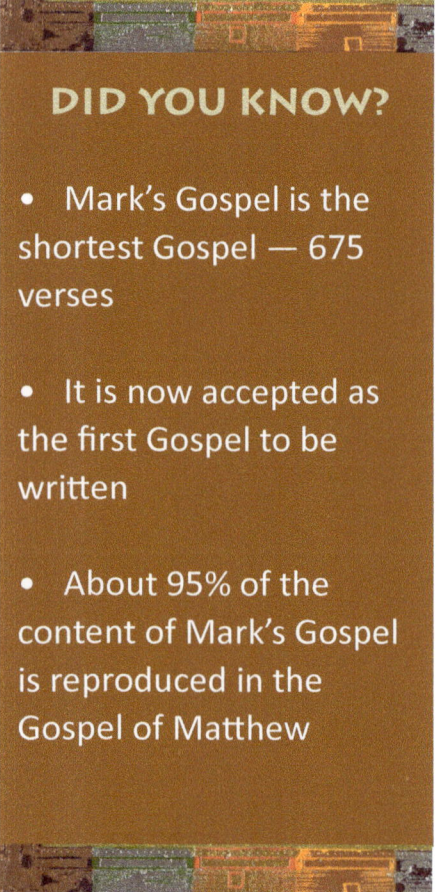

DID YOU KNOW?

- Mark's Gospel is the shortest Gospel — 675 verses

- It is now accepted as the first Gospel to be written

- About 95% of the content of Mark's Gospel is reproduced in the Gospel of Matthew

JESUS AND THE DISCIPLES

The most important 'character' in the story of Jesus told by Mark is Jesus. The early Christians already had a memory of his life and ministry, but it had never been written down like this before. More than that, it had never been called 'good news'. The English word 'gospel' is a translation of a Greek word that means 'good news'. Indeed, 'gospel' comes from an Old English word (*god-spel*) that also means 'good news'. There are very few scenes in Mark's story where Jesus is not at the centre of the action. From the early stages of the Gospel (see 1:16–20), Jesus calls others to join him. He asks a group of people to 'follow' him. They are his disciples, and from among them he appoints a smaller group: 'the twelve' (see 3:13–19).

The relationship between Jesus and the disciples is crucial for the message that Mark wishes to communicate through his story. As we attempt to follow Jesus in our own time, we can identify with the disciples in the story. Towards the end of the story a group of women begin to play an increasingly important role. Their role is closely associated with the disciples. Indeed, as we will see, they succeed where the male disciples fail. Mark's story presents a vivid picture of Jesus and the disciples. The disciples and the chosen Twelve respond generously and willingly (1:16–20; 2:17; 3:13–19). In the early part of the story, they share willingly in his ministry, as they witness his miracles, and listen to his preaching (see chapters 4 and 5).

However, they wonder who he might be, and Jesus expresses, for the first time, his disappointment in them (4:40–41). Nevertheless, a high point is reached, after the disciples ask further questions about Jesus which continue to

disappoint him, when he asks them at Caesarea Philippi who they think he is. The belief of the disciples is expressed in the words of Peter: 'You are the Christ' (NRSV: 'Messiah') (8:29). The reader knows from the very first line in the story (1:1) that this is a correct understanding of Jesus, but there are different ways of understanding what it means to be 'the Christ'. There is a danger that the disciples might think that Jesus is an all-powerful conquering hero, come to save Israel from the Roman occupation, and to restore the Davidic kingdom.

The story has reached a turning point. Immediately following Peter's confession, Jesus begins to speak about his response to God as the Son of Man who must suffer many things, be killed and on the third day rise again (8:31). Across the second half of the story, as Jesus journeys towards Jerusalem with his disciples, he repeats this prediction on two further occasions (9:31; 10:32–34), and the disciples begin to experience fear and disappointment about what might lie ahead of them (10:32). But he does not abandon them. He calls them to himself and instructs them on the need to take up their own cross, to abandon all pretensions of grandeur and success so that they might be servants. They are followers of the Son of Man who came, not to be served, but to serve (10:45).

At a final meal, the night before he dies, he predicts that one of them will betray him, another will deny him, and that all the rest will abandon him as they flee from danger. But in the midst of these predictions of failure, he gives himself to them in the broken bread and the shared wine of a meal that is the foreshadowing of all the Eucharistic celebrations since that night. Jesus goes on giving himself unconditionally, out of love for his disciples from all eras who never love him in the way he has loved us (14:17–25).

Jesus' predictions come true.

> *Follow me and I will make you fish for people.*

Judas betrays him, Peter denies him, and all the disciples flee in fear. In the original version of the Gospel of Mark that ends at 16:8, the brief announcement that all the disciples deserted him and fled (14:50) marks the final appearance of the disciples as a collective group of 'characters' who were chosen by Jesus to follow him. Peter does make an appearance later in chapter 14 as an individual, not as a follower of Jesus.

But at the empty tomb the young man tells the women that Jesus is no longer where he was laid after his death. He has been raised by God, and they are to announce this Easter message to the disciples and Peter. Jesus is going ahead of them into Galilee. There they will see him, as he had told them (16:6–7). The story of a relationship between Jesus, now the risen Jesus, and his disciples, is about to begin again, despite their failure, in Galilee. This is where it began; this is where it will be resumed. But the women, like the disciples, are so struck with fear that they run away and do not say anything to anyone (16:8).

This is where the original Gospel closed. Later scribes, unhappy with this ending, so different to the endings of Matthew 28, Luke 24 and John 20, added a longer ending (16:9–20). But Mark's surprising story ends with Jesus' words, first uttered at the last meal (14:28), ringing out again: 'He is going ahead of you to Galilee; there you will see him' (16:7). For Mark, and for believing Christians, the word of Jesus does not fail. He is going before them into Galilee. Discipleship goes on, not because the original disciples or even the more courageous women succeeded. We are contemporary Christians because God meets us in his Son, going before us, despite our failures, into the Galilee of our future as he did with the original disciples. There we shall see him.

DID YOU KNOW?

• 'Christ' is a title given to Jesus, not part of his name. It comes from the Greek word *Christos* meaning 'anointed'. This has the same meaning as 'Messiah', which is Hebrew in origin

• Peter's declaration about Jesus: 'You are the Christ' (8:29) is a central moment in the Gospel

• Jesus instructs the disciples to be silent about Peter's words because he is concerned that his message will be interpreted in a political rather than spiritual way

Mark's way of telling the story of Jesus

The four different Gospel stories of Jesus are one of the great treasures of the Christian tradition. There can never be 'one story' that captures the breadth and depth of the mystery of what God has done for us in and through his Son, Jesus Christ. We are privileged to have *four stories* regarded by Christian tradition as 'inspired' as part of our sacred Scriptures. Our task is to single out and try to understand the *uniqueness* of the story of Jesus as Mark told it, and to see the riches that this particular story brings into our understanding of Jesus, and of ourselves.

The Gospel of Mark is the shortest, but in some ways the most challenging, of the four Gospels. From what we have already seen in tracing the relationship between Jesus and the disciples in the Gospel, it is clear that there are at least two parts to the Gospel. The first is set in Galilee, and it closes with Peter's confession that Jesus is the Christ, and Jesus' prohibiting the disciples to say anything about this (8:29–30). The rest of the story has Jesus and the disciples either 'on the way' to Jerusalem, or in Jerusalem. The second half of the story tells the surprising message that Jesus can only be the Messiah and the Son of God as the suffering and dying Son of Man who will be raised by God. It is predicted (see 8:31; 9:31; 10:32–34) and then acted out in the account of Jesus' suffering, death and resurrection (14:1 – 16:8).

These two major sections of the story can be further refined. The Gospel begins with a short section, dedicated to the figure of John the Baptist and his baptism of Jesus, at the end of which *the reader or listener* has been fully introduced to the mystery of the person of Jesus. Like Matthew 1:1 – 4:16,

Luke 1:1 – 4:13 and John 1:1–18, Mark 1:1–13 serves as a 'prologue' to the Gospel of Mark. Only the reader and the listener become aware of what is revealed in Mark 1:1–13. The characters in the story, especially the disciples, but also all the other characters (crowds, Romans, Jesus' family, and certain individuals who encounter Jesus [for example, the rich man, the scribe, the Pharisees, the Sadducees and Pilate]) *have not read the prologue of Mark 1:1–13*.

The first half of Jesus' story in Mark, set in Galilee, tells of Jesus' ministry, bringing in the reigning presence of God as King ('the Kingdom of God'). His teaching, his miracles and his encounters with others make people wonder who he might be. In fact, there are three groups of people whose close encounter with Jesus is recorded in Mark 1:13 – 8:30. From 1:13 to 3:6 Jesus clashes with the Jewish leaders. This section closes with their plan to kill him (3:6). From 3:7 to 6:6a Jesus establishes a new family that replaces his natural, blood family, and he instructs them by parables and through his miracles (4:1 – 5:43). This section closes when the people from his own town reject him, and Jesus is astounded at their lack of belief in him (6:1–6a). The final section is dominated by the association of the disciples with the ministry of Jesus, especially highlighted by the two bread miracles (6:31–44; 8:1–9). It closes at Caesarea Philippi, with Peter's confession, in the name of all the disciples, that Jesus is the Christ, and Jesus' warning that they should not speak about this (8:29–30).

As in 1:13 – 8:30, there are three sections to the second half of the Gospel. They tell and then show that he is Messiah and Son of God as a suffering and victorious Son of Man. As the section that closed the first half of the Gospel focused on the disciples, the first section of the second half is dedicated almost entirely to Jesus' attempt to lead them from blindness to sight (see the hint in 8:22–26). But they will not and cannot accept that he will be Messiah only as a suffering Son of Man (8:31 – 10:52). The second section begins as Jesus enters Jerusalem. There we find a series of 'endings'. Jesus brings to an end Temple worship (11:1–27) and the Jewish institutions (11:28 – 12:44), and he speaks of the end of Jerusalem and the end of the world (13:1–37). The third of the three sections is made up of the story of Jesus' trials, suffering and death (14:1 – 15:46). At his death a Roman centurion, the first human being in the story to make a full confession of faith, looks at how Jesus died, and announces that Jesus was truly the Son of God (15:39).

I do not include the account of Jesus' resurrection in the second half of the Gospel story because I regard the events reported in 16:1–8, at the empty tomb, as being directed to disciples of all times. Just as the prologue of 1:1–13 was directed only to the listener and the reader, the enigmatic ending of Mark's account of the empty tomb also asks questions of the disciple. As the women have fled in fear, and said nothing to anyone, how is Jesus' promise that he is going before his disciples into Galilee, and that there they will see him, fulfilled (16:7–8)? It is fulfilled in the lives of all subsequent disciples who have read or listened to this Gospel. They guarantee that Jesus' promise to be with us in Galilee comes true. I therefore suggest that 16:1–8 serves as an 'epilogue' challenging the readers and listeners, just as the 'prologue' (1:1–13) challenged the readers and the listeners. The epilogue may appear at the end of the story, but it is a promise of a new beginning.

More schematically, what I have just written looks like this:

1. Prologue: the beginning (1:1–13)
2. The mystery of Jesus (1:14 – 8:30)
   a. Jesus and the leaders of Israel (1:14 – 3:6)
   b. Jesus and his new family (3:7 – 6:6a)
   c. Jesus and his disciples (6:6b – 8:30)
3. The suffering and vindicated Son of Man: Jesus is Christ and Son of God (8:31 – 15:47)
   a. Leading the disciples from blindness to sight (8:31 – 10:52)
   b. The symbolic end of Israel and the world (11:1 – 13:37)
   c. The crucifixion and death of Jesus, Son of Man, Christ and Son of God (14:1 – 15:47)
4. Epilogue: a new beginning (16:1–8).

As I 'tell the story', I will pause from time to time to devote a little more attention to major passages for our understanding of Jesus and what it means to be his disciple, and to other passages that serve as dramatic turning points in the story.

DID YOU KNOW?

- The Gospels of Matthew, Mark and Luke have much in common but each tells the story of Jesus in a slightly different way

- Each Gospel was written for a particular group to address particular needs

- The way each story is told reflects the major religious and social problems each community had to face

The prologue: Mark 1:1–13

All the Gospels have a prologue. This means that when the reader has come to the end of the prologue, she or he has had a clear idea of *who* Jesus is and *what* he has done. This is the case for the prologues of all the Gospels. Where they differ is in what follows. Each Gospel has a different way of telling Jesus' life to show — by means of God's gracious and surprising action in our human story — *how* Jesus was the Son of God, Messiah and Saviour.

The first part of verses 1 to 13 is dedicated to John the Baptist, but two voices speak in verses 1 to 3. The first voice is the authoritative voice of Mark, announcing the beginning of the 'good news' that Jesus is the Christ and the Son of God (v 1). The use of the expression 'beginning' has two meanings. Mark tells his readers that they are at the beginning of a story. But he also looks back to another 'beginning', the beginning of God's creating presence, recorded in the Book of Genesis, which also opened with the word 'beginning'. The good news is that Jesus is the Christ and the Son of God, and a new creation is at hand. The second voice speaks: the Word *of God* (vv 2–3). Speaking through his prophet Isaiah, God announces that he will send a messenger to prepare the way of 'the Lord'. The good news that follows will be about Jesus, Christ, Son of God and Lord.

The second stage in the prologue is reported by Mark (vv 4–6). John the Baptist does not come

Mark 1:1–13

1 The beginning of the good news of Jesus Christ, the Son of God.
2 As it is written in the prophet Isaiah,
"See, I am sending my messenger ahead of you,
   who will prepare your way;
3 the voice of one crying out in the wilderness:
   'Prepare the way of the Lord,
   make his paths straight,' "
4 John the baptizer appeared in the wilderness, proclaiming a baptism of repentance for the forgiveness of sins. 5 And people from the whole Judean countryside and all the people of Jerusalem were going out to him, and were baptized by him in the river Jordan, confessing their sins. 6 Now John was clothed with camel's hair, with a leather belt around his waist, and he ate locusts and wild honey. 7 He proclaimed, "The one who is more powerful than I is coming after me; I am not worthy to stoop down and untie the thong of his sandals. 8 I have baptized you with water; but he will baptize you with the Holy Spirit."

9 In those days Jesus came from Nazareth of Galilee and was baptized by John in the Jordan. 10 And just as he was coming up out of the water, he saw the heavens torn apart and the Spirit descending like a dove on him. 11 And a voice came from heaven, "You are my Son, the Beloved; with you I am well pleased."

12 And the Spirit immediately drove him out into the wilderness. 13 He was in the wilderness forty days, tempted by Satan; and he was with the wild beasts; and the angels waited on him.

into the action. Mark tells of the partial fulfilment of God's promise in the announcement, appearance and description of the forerunner, the one who is to prepare the way. Next the Baptist speaks (vv 7–8). He announces the coming of the one 'more powerful', one before whom the forerunner is totally unworthy. The stronger one 'will baptize you with the Holy Spirit'. He is preparing the way for 'the Lord'.

The focus shifts again as the Baptist continues to be the main actor in the story, but Jesus is introduced (vv 9–11). Though Jesus does nothing, the promise of the voice of God that the coming of 'the Lord' is at hand is fulfilled. He is baptised by John, and as he comes up out of the water the heavens open. God enters the story when the firmament that separates heaven from earth splits open: God's Spirit, with which Jesus will baptise, descends upon Jesus from above. A divine voice speaks directly to Jesus: 'You are my Son, the Beloved; with you I am well pleased' (v 11).

Mark next reports that the divine Spirit drives Jesus into the wilderness (v 12). Present there for forty days, Jesus is tempted by Satan, and the angels minister to him. At the end of the prologue Jesus acts: 'he was with the wild beasts' (v 13). The hint of a new creation in verse 1 ('the beginning') returns in verses 12 to 13. In the Genesis story Satan's victory over Adam led to hostility and fear in creation (see Gen 3:14–21; Ps 91:11–13). Mark began the account of the ministry, death and resurrection of Jesus with a suggestion that this situation has been reversed: he was *with* the wild beasts. Prophetic traditions surrounding the new creation are fulfilled (see Isa 11:6–9; 35:3–10; Ezek 34:23–31). A link with creation themes is also found in the presence of the angels serving Jesus. Repeatedly throughout the desert experience of Israel angels help and guide the wandering people (see Ex 14:19; 23:20, 23; 32:34; 33:2). During Elijah's experience of hunger and despair in the wilderness, he is served by angels

> And just as he was coming up out of the water, he saw the heavens and the Spirit descending and a voice came from heaven

(1 Kings 19:5–7). Although not present in the biblical account, Jewish documents speculate that Adam and Eve were fed by the angels in the Garden of Eden.

Only towards the end of the prologue does the hint of the link with the original creation return, provided by the word 'beginning' of verse 1. Jesus is 'with the wild beasts' and 'waited on' by the angels. His coming restores the original order of God's creation. Jesus has been *presented* to the reader. He is the Christ, the Son of God (v 1), the Lord (v 3) and the more powerful one (v 7), who will baptise with the Holy Spirit (v 8). God's voice has assured us that Jesus is the beloved Son of God, and that God is well pleased with him (v 11). He is filled with the Spirit (v 10), and driven into the desert to reverse the tragedy of Adam and Eve, to re-establish God's original design (vv 12–13).

There should be no doubt in the reader's mind about *who Jesus is*. However, there are hints throughout the prologue that point to a ministry, if he is to baptise with the Holy Spirit (v 8). There is perhaps a hint that he will be sacrificed as God's 'beloved', in a way similar to Isaac, the beloved son of Abraham (v 11; see Gen 22:1–19). Mark wants the reader to arrive at the end of the prologue well informed about *who* Jesus is, but as yet unaware of *how* Jesus is the Christ, the Son of God, the Lord and the Stronger One who baptises with the Holy Spirit, and *how* in his person God's original creative design is to be restored. All early Christians knew that Jesus of Nazareth was crucified, and they may well have questioned how such an end could be pleasing to God (see v 11). Mark has written a story that attempts to respond to that question.

DID YOU KNOW?

• Jesus' baptism by John marks the beginning of Jesus' ministry in all four Gospels

• Although based in authentic memories of the life and teaching of Jesus, the Gospels are not biographies of Jesus, as we understand the term 'biography' today

• The first verse of Mark's Gospel proclaims that this is not a life story but 'good news' that Jesus is the Christ and the Son of God

torn apart like a dove on him. You are my Son, the Beloved; with you I am well pleased.'

THE MYSTERY OF JESUS: MARK 1:14 – 8:30

1 — Jesus and the Leaders of Israel (1:14 – 3:6)

Mark 1:14 – 8:30, dedicated to an unravelling of the mystery of Jesus, is located in its entirety in Galilee. This ministry has three major moments. Each section begins with a *brief summary* of Jesus' ministry and ends with a *decision* about Jesus. Mark 1:14 – 3:6 opens with one of the most important summaries in the Gospel (1:14–15): 'Now after John was arrested, Jesus came to Galilee, proclaiming the good news of God, and saying, "The time is fulfilled, and the Kingdom of God has come near; repent, and believe in the good news."' It closes with a decision to kill Jesus, as 'The Pharisees went out and immediately conspired with the Herodians against him, how to destroy him' (3:6). Between the summary (1:14–15) and the decision (3:6), the action happens rapidly. Mark uses the Greek word for 'immediately' so often that we leave it out of much of our translation. But it insinuates urgency into Jesus' story, and his unconditional response to his Father. Hard on the heels of the summary of verses 14 and 15, Jesus calls his first disciples (1:16–20). *Immediately* he calls others to follow, and they respond without hesitation, following him down his way. Responding to Jesus' call, they follow him wordlessly, leaving behind all that their peer group would regard as signs of their success: their boats, their nets, their hired servants and their father (vv 16–20).

Following the call of the first disciples, Jesus overcomes various powers of evil. The first is an unclean spirit in the synagogue at

Capernaum on a Sabbath (v 21). As Jesus teaches and generates wonder over his authority, an unclean spirit speaks out. This spirit recognises who Jesus is ('the Holy one of God') and should thus be able to command him (vv 22–24). However, Jesus dismisses the unclean spirit, leading everyone to wonder who Jesus might be, and the gradual spread of his name in the region (vv 25–28).

Jesus next overcomes sickness and taboo as he touches Simon's mother-in-law, heals her and is served by her (vv 29–31). No religious man would touch the body of a woman he did not know, nor be served at table by her. Jesus does both and overcomes evil by his touch and presence. Mark summarises Jesus' healing activity and his power over demons (vv 32–34), as Jesus goes to a lonely place to pray (v 35). But Simon and some of the disciples disturb Jesus in his prayer. They want him to go back to the place of his wondrous activity and acclaim, but this is not what God, his Father, is asking of him. Jesus' mission will not come to an end until he reaches Jerusalem. He accepts this as the design of God, announcing, 'For that is what I came out to do' (v 38c).

Jesus resumes his response to the design of God, with whom he has been briefly joined in prayer. He journeys throughout all Galilee, preaching and casting out demons (vv 36–39). Finally, the power and goodness of the reigning presence

12 A FRIENDLY GUIDE TO MARK'S GOSPEL

of God cuts through ritual taboo, as Jesus responds with affection to a leper and heals him with a command (vv 40–41). After instructing the former leper to indicate to the religious authority that he is now clean and fit to take up his place among the people, Jesus asks the man to say nothing about this wonderful event (vv 43–44). There is a danger that people might get the wrong idea about Jesus. They might suspect that he is a miracle-working Messiah. Jesus' messiahship cannot be understood without the cross and thus he commands silence, as he will continue to do throughout the early part of the story. But the former leper announces far and wide what Jesus has done, which meant that Jesus must stay out in the country, but people still came to him (v 45).

Jesus' proclamation in verse 15 is bearing fruit. The presence of the Kingdom *of God* is rendering powerless the signs of the kingdom *of evil*: sickness, taboo and unclean spirits evaporate before him, vanquished by his authoritative word (vv 25, 39, 41) and touch (vv 31, 41). The mystery of Jesus is among them: 'What is this? A new teaching — with authority! He commands even the unclean spirits, and they obey him' (v 27). The time is fulfilled; there is repentance, and the power of the reigning presence of God is at hand (v 15).

This situation, however, does not last. The first moments of Jesus' ministry are directed against *the powers of evil*, and they are unable to withstand his presence. But such is not the case in the encounter between the word, works and person of Jesus and *the leaders of Israel*. The five episodes in 2:1 – 3:6 not only report the spread of Jesus' ongoing authority, but also a mounting rejection of this authority. This is evident in Mark's carefully planned series of episodes, surrounding a central episode in 2:18–22.

A **2:1–12** Jesus *enters* Capernaum *again* (see 3:1), and forgives *the sins* of a paralytic, but 'some of the scribes' *in their hearts* question Jesus' authority to forgive *sin* (see also vv 9, 10). He affirms this authority by *raising* (v 11; see also vv 9, 12) the paralytic.

B **2:13–17** Jesus calls Levi from his tax office, and shares his table and *eats* (v 16a; see also v 16b) with similarly situated characters — sinners and tax collectors — along with his disciples. 'The scribes of the Pharisees' complain about such behaviour *to his disciples*.

C **2:18–22** At a time when the disciples of the Baptist and the Pharisees are *fasting* (v 18a; see vv 18b, 19, 20), 'people' *came to him* and asked why he did not fast like other religious people. For the first time in the story, the death of Jesus is predicted. For the moment Jesus is with them, and there is no need for the wedding guests to fast. The biblical theme of the great messianic meal, when the bridegroom of Israel comes to take possession of his bride, indicates that the Messiah is with them, and there is no call for fasting. However, there is a time coming in the near future when this situation will be changed by the violence of those who oppose Jesus. The wedding guests will eventually fast when the bridegroom is *taken away* from them (v 20). This centrepiece of the section dedicated to the growing conflict between Jesus and the leaders of Israel (2:1 – 3:6) closes with some of the most radical words of Jesus in the Gospel of Mark. Jesus makes two comparisons. No one sews a piece of new cloth onto an old cloak. No one pours new wine into old wineskins. The addition of the new to the old only destroys both. What Jesus has come to bring is entirely new, and it simply cannot be contained in old wineskins (vv 21–22). But this newness will only be made possible by the cross (v 20).

B¹ **2:23–28** As Jesus and his disciples pluck grain and eat *on a Sabbath*, 'the Pharisees' *question Jesus* on the right observance of the Law, only to be instructed on Abiathar's *eating* the bread of the Presence (v 26a; see also v 26b).

A¹ **3:1–6** *On a Sabbath*, a man with a withered hand is present as Jesus *enters* the synagogue *again* (see 2:1). But 'they' were watching to see what he would do on the holy day so that '*they might accuse him*'. He reduces them to silence, grieves over the *hardness of their hearts* (v 5), *raises* the maimed man (v 3) and performs the miracle (v 5). The Pharisees and the Herodians hold counsel: how to destroy him.

Mark 2:18–22

18 Now John's disciples and the Pharisees were fasting; and people came and said to him, "Why do John's disciples and the disciples of the Pharisees fast, but your disciples do not fast?" 19 Jesus said to them, "The wedding guests cannot fast while the bridegroom is with them, can they? As long as they have the bridegroom with them, they cannot fast. 20 The days will come when the bridegroom is taken away from them, and then they will fast on that day."

21 "No one sews a piece of unshrunk cloth on an old cloak; otherwise, the patch pulls away from it, the new from the old, and a worse tear is made. 22 And no one puts new wine into old wineskins; otherwise, the wine will burst the skins, and the wine is lost, and so are the skins; but one puts new wine into fresh wineskins."

I have highlighted words in this outline of 2:1 – 3:6 to show how the episodes relate to one another. (see boxed text on page 13) The reported events all contain conflict between Jesus and leading figures in Israel. At the beginning and end of these five episodes (2:1–12 and 3:1–6), Mark reports Jesus' entry into a town and a synagogue. On both occasions — but nowhere in the intervening three episodes (2:13–28) — he works a miracle. Both stories refer to 'raising' (see 2:9, 11, 12; 3:3). Mark has framed the five episodes with episodes that show the ongoing power of God's reigning presence, and the authority of Jesus, despite the opposition of the leaders of Israel.

The second and the fourth episodes (2:13–17 and 2:23–28) both focus upon the theme of eating, and in each episode objections from the Jewish leadership is overcome by Jesus' teaching and his affirmation of his authority. At the very centre of the five episodes (2:18–22: the third episode), the opposite of eating is the theme: fasting. The time will come when the bridegroom will be taken away. This is the first hint of Jesus' violent death at the hands of the people who are opposing him. It is the central message of 2:1 – 3:6, contrasting with the references to 'raising' in the first and last episodes (2:1–12; 3:1–6). The first passage is picked up and repeated in the final passage (A and A[1]), the second re-stated in the fourth (B and B[1]), and the central message is provided for the reader in the third episode (C).

The five episodes indicate a *mounting opposition* to Jesus. His opponents initially object 'in their hearts' (2:6). They speak to the disciples (v 16), then to Jesus (v 18). They dispute Sabbath Law with Jesus (v 24). Finally, in silence they watch in the hope that they might find something with which to accuse him (3:2), and plot his destruction (v 6). There is a similar growth in the people who oppose Jesus. Representatives of Israel are included in descriptions of the opponents: scribes (2:8), scribes of the Pharisees (v 16), people (v 18), the Pharisees (v 24), 'they' (3:2), and the Pharisees and the Herodians (v 6). But, despite the opposition, there is also an ongoing development of the presentation of the authority of Jesus and his teaching. The first two episodes deal with sin and sinners (2:1–12, 13–17), and in the final two episodes Jesus

performs actions that question a traditional understanding of the Sabbath (2:23–28; 3:1–6). The unveiling of Jesus' role and authority also develops from the first miracle, where the Son of Man is shown to have authority to forgive sins (2:10), to the two final scenes where the Son of Man declares he is lord of the Sabbath (2:28; 3:2).

Mark introduces the shadow of the cross for the first time: 'The days will come when the bridegroom is taken away from them' (2:20), and that day is already being plotted as Pharisees and Herodians plan his destruction (3:6). Through all amazed and glorified God' (2:12). Yet Jesus forbids the demons, who know who he is, to speak (1:34) and insists that his deeds not become the focus of attention (1:44). Mark 1:14 – 3:6 vigorously addresses the question of Jesus' identity. Regardless of the mounting opposition to Jesus across 2:1 – 3:6, Jesus continues to proclaim the kingdom, and people stream to him from every corner (3:7–8; see 1:45). The first major series of episodes in Mark's story announces that Jesus' presence to Israel has not been fruitless, despite the leaders' decision that he must be destroyed.

(6:1–6a). As in 1:14 – 3:6 (see 1:16–20), Mark adds a discipleship story to the summary. Jesus calls disciples (v 13) and appoints the Twelve to be with him to do the things that Jesus has done: he will send them out to preach and to have authority to cast out demons (vv 14–15). The Twelve are named (vv 16–19), a group who will 'be with him' (3:14).

With his disciples, in 3:20–25 Jesus turns to face the misunderstanding, the hostility and the rejection of those who were 'his own'. Jesus goes home (v 20a). People flock to him and his family express concern for his sanity (vv 20b–21).

these episodes Mark continues to show an increasing interest and wonder in Jesus' person. Characters in the story who have not read the prologue encounter Jesus and raise questions: 'What is this? A new teaching … !' (1:27); 'Everyone is searching for you' (v 37); 'We have never seen anything like this!' (2:12); 'They were astounded at his teaching' (1:22); 'His fame began to spread' (v 28); 'And the whole city was gathered around the door' (v 33); 'People came to him from every quarter' (v 45); and 'They were

II — JESUS AND HIS NEW FAMILY (3:7 – 6:6A)

This second part of Mark's story of the mystery of Jesus again opens with a summary in 3:7–12. People from every quarter receive him (vv 7–8). He effects cures and drives out evil spirits who know who he is (vv 9–10). They are commanded to silence (vv 11–12). It will end with a decision from his own townsfolk that he has nothing to offer, as they know his family

As well as his 'blood family', his 'religious and ethnic family' has difficulties with who he is and what he is teaching. The scribes from Jerusalem deny the source of Jesus' authority. It cannot come from God; it must be from the powers of evil. Jesus points out their error and condemns them as guilty of an eternal sin. Anyone who cannot accept that the Son of God works in the power of the Spirit denies the Spirit. This decision places them in a situation where forgiveness is impossible (vv 22–30).

Who is the true family of Jesus? In verses 31 to 35 his mother and his brothers and sisters come to him while he is teaching. He tells those listening to him that his family are 'outside', while those 'inside' are listening to him. He solemnly establishes a new criterion for belonging to his family: doing the will of God (vv 31–35). Mark has carefully placed passages that deal with Jesus' blood family (vv 20–21 and vv 31–35) around other passages where he encounters his national and religious family (vv 22–30). Jesus turns away from the established criteria for being a member of the family of Jesus. By means of verses 20 to 35 a new criterion for 'belonging' to Jesus emerges: 'Whoever does the will of God' (v 35).

Jesus begins his longest sequence of teaching in the Gospel. Expressions from the verb 'to teach' appear three times in the first two verses (4:1–2) as Jesus uses a boat as a pulpit, initially to tell the crowds the parable of the sown seed (vv 3–9). But after the parable he withdraws with his disciples and indicates to them that they have been chosen. They are privileged 'insiders' (vv 10–13). He proceeds to explain the meaning of the parable of the sown seed to them (vv 14–20). The privileged insiders, who struggle to understand Jesus' teaching, are challenged by the parable of the light under a bushel (vv 21–25). What they have received must be seen, and not hidden. Jesus turns back to address the larger assembly in two short parables of the growing seed (vv 26–29) and the mustard seed (vv 30–32). They build upon the theme of 'growth' that is present through all the parables. However small and insignificant, however oppressed (see 2:1 – 3:6), the kingdom preached by Jesus will blossom and bear fruit. Mark closes this section with the comment, 'With many such parables he spoke the word to them, as they were able to hear it; he did not speak to them except in parables, but he explained everything in private to his disciples' (vv 33–34). The primary focus of Jesus' attention throughout his teaching is his new family, those who are 'inside' and to whom have been given the gift of the mystery of the reigning presence of God (see vv 11–13).

Having taught his new family in parables, they now witness a series of miracles (4:35 – 5:43). The miracles happen in rapid succession to show, in the first place, the power of Jesus' presence, and secondly, the difficulty that the disciples experience in accepting and understanding the full significance of this presence. The miracles open with victory over the stormy seas (vv 35–41). Jesus calms the seas, while the disciples tremble with fear, and ask: 'Who then is this, that even the wind and the sea obey him?' (v 41). This is the first sign of the fragility of the disciples. After having courageously left all they had in order to follow him (1:16–20) and having been side by side with him through the first days of his ministry, with their miracles and conflicts (1:21 – 3:6), they are filled with fear, and wonder who he might be.

Jesus moves into Gerasa, a Gentile land, and drives out the Legion of unclean spirits. In doing so, he also purifies the land, sending the unclean pigs into the destruction of the sea (5:1–20). When the villagers come to see who had done this deed, and wish to know what had happened, it is most likely the disciples who inform them: 'Those who had seen what had happened to the demoniac and to the swine reported it' (v 16). The cured man asks 'to be with him [Jesus]'

(v 18; see 3:14), but Jesus has other plans for him. He is sent off to his village to proclaim what the Lord has done for him, and he does so, proclaiming what *Jesus* had done for him (vv 19–20). He is the first person in the Gospel of Mark to preach Jesus in a Gentile land.

In the combined account of the woman with the flow of blood and the raising of Jairus's daughter, Jesus overcomes human sickness, and even death (5:21–43).

(see boxed text right)
The 'pairing' of these two miracle stories is one of Mark's favourite literary techniques, often called a 'sandwich construction'. Mark wants the reader to understand these two miracles in the light of one another: the Jairus story provides the frame (5:21–24a, 35–43), and the story of the woman with the flow of blood lies at the centre (vv 24b–34). He opens the narrative with the approach of Jairus and his humble prostration before Jesus, requesting a cure for his daughter (5:21–24a). On the way to the home of Jairus, the woman who has had a flow of blood *for twelve years* also approaches Jesus, believing that his touch would cure her. Feeling her touch, Jesus asks who touched him, and is ridiculed *by his disciples* for such a question as so many people are thronging about him (v 31). The courageous woman comes forward, and Jesus assures her that her faith has made her whole (vv 24b–34), and that she can go in peace (vv 24b–34). Proceeding to the home of Jairus, Jesus is again ridiculed by the mourners when he announces that the child is only asleep. He sends them away, *takes her by the hand* and summons her to rise. She rises from the dead, and Jesus insists that she be fed and that this story not be spread abroad.

Mark 5:21–43

21 When Jesus had crossed again in the boat to the other side, a great crowd gathered around him; and he was by the sea. 22 Then one of the leaders of the synagogue named Jairus came and, when he saw him, fell at his feet 23 and begged him repeatedly, "My little daughter is at the point of death. Come and lay your hands on her, so that she may be made well, and live." 24 So he went with him. And a large crowd followed him and pressed in on him. 25 Now there was a woman who had been suffering from hemorrhages for twelve years. 26 She had endured much under many physicians, and had spent all that she had; and she was no better, but rather grew worse. 27 She had heard about Jesus, and came up behind him in the crowd and touched his cloak, 28 for she said, "If I but touch his clothes, I will be made well." 29 Immediately her hemorrhage stopped; and she felt in her body that she was healed of her disease. 30 Immediately aware that power had gone forth from him, Jesus turned about in the crowd and said, "Who touched my clothes?" 31 And his disciples said to him, "You see the crowd pressing in on you; how can you say, 'Who touched me?' " 32 He looked all around to see who had done it. 33 But the woman, knowing what had happened to her, came in fear and trembling, fell down before him, and told him the whole truth. 34 He said to her, "Daughter, your faith has made you well; go in peace, and be healed of your disease."

35 While he was still speaking, some people came from the leader's house to say, "Your daughter is dead. Why trouble the teacher any further?" 36 But overhearing what they said, Jesus said to the leader of the synagogue, "Do not fear, only believe." 37 He allowed no one to follow him except Peter, James, and John, the brother of James. 38 When they came to the house of the leader of the synagogue, he saw a commotion, people weeping and wailing loudly. 39 When he had entered, he said to them, "Why do you make a commotion and weep? The child is not dead but sleeping." 40 And they laughed at him. Then he put them all outside, and took the child's father and mother and those who were with him, and went in where the child was. 41 He took her by the hand and said to her, "Talitha cum," which means, "Little girl, get up!" 42 And immediately the girl got up and began to walk about (she was twelve years of age). At this they were overcome with amazement. 43 He strictly ordered them that no one should know this, and told them to give her something to eat.

The power and authority of Jesus overcome sickness and death, and the faith of Jairus and the woman with the flow of blood restore health, life and peace to the afflicted. Jesus allows himself to be *touched* by a woman who was perpetually ritually unclean. By his touch he restores her to wholeness and peace (v 34). Similarly, he *touches* a dead girl *of twelve years of age* (v 42). If she is dead, then he renders himself impure by touching a dead body; if she is only asleep, then he touches a young woman who is marriageable. Yet his touch restores her to life. Both women are restored to wholeness and peace because they have been 'touched' by God's reigning presence in and through the person of Jesus. But the disciples and others find Jesus' healing and life-giving presence hard to understand and accept (see vv 31, 40).

The second section of Jesus' Galilean ministry (3:7 – 6:6a) also leads to a decision about him (see 3:6). He returns to his hometown, followed by his disciples (6:1). The people from his hometown ask about the source of his wisdom (see 4:1–34: his parables) and his mighty power (see 4:35 – 5:53: his miracles) (v 2). They give the wrong answer. They know his mother and his brothers and sisters (vv 3–5). We, who have read the prologue (1:1–13), are aware that Jesus' wisdom and power reflect the reigning presence *of God*, but Jesus' townsfolk cannot see beyond his blood family. Jesus is amazed at their lack of faith, and is rendered powerless among them (v 6a).

Jesus' Galilean ministry continues in 3:7 – 6:6a, but the storyteller's focus upon the new family of Jesus is unmistakable. His blood family and his fellow Jews, either consider him insane (3:20–21), driven by the prince of evil spirits (3:22–30), or of no consequence, as they know his mother, brothers and sisters (6:1–6a). Faced by this opposition and rejection, Jesus teaches by means of parables and miracles (4:1 – 5:43), but explains their deeper meaning to his new family, the disciples (4:10–13; 14–20, 33–34), 'insiders', specially gifted with the mystery of the Kingdom of God (4:11).

III — JESUS AND THE DISCIPLES (6:6B – 8:30)

Jesus' rejection (6:1–6a) leads to one of the briefest summaries in the Gospel, 'Then he went about among the villages teaching' (6:6b). Mark 6:6b is also followed by dealings with the disciples (vv 7–30). The mission of the disciples in verses 7 to 13 opens another 'sandwich construction'. The Twelve are 'sent out' to continue the work of Jesus, teaching with authority, healing the sick and driving out demons (vv 7–13), but while they are on the mission, Mark tells of the death of John the Baptist (vv 14–29). As a messenger of God who announces Jesus, the Baptist has an unswerving commitment to his mission. It costs him his life (6:17–29). His life and death have close parallels with the life and death of Jesus who is also put to death by a ruler who recognises his goodness (see 15:9–10, 12, 14 [Jesus] and 6:20, 26 [John the Baptist]), but who

Overhearing what they said, Jesus said to the leader of the synagogue, 'Do not fear, only believe.'

succumbed to pressure (see 15:10, 14–15 [Jesus] and 6:22–26 [John the Baptist]). Jesus announces the present and future coming of God, cost what it may (15:48; 16:60–62), and the Baptist stands by his God-given task, continuing his call to repentance and forgiveness even into the court of the King (6:17–19). For both of them, it leads to death. But when the disciples 'sent out' return, they are full of the success of their teaching and of the wonders they have done. They are moving into an arrogant world of their own (6:30).

Mark shapes the remainder of this part of the story around two bread miracles (6:31–44; 8:1–10), and a series of repeated events that follow each of the bread miracles. There are two boat trips (6:45–56; 8:10), two conflicts (7:1–23; 8:11–21) and two healing miracles (7:24–37; 8:22–26) following each bread miracle. In 6:31–44 Mark reports *the first multiplication of the loaves and fish*. The story indicates that this miracle takes place in Israel, on the Jewish side of the lake. The Eucharistic celebrations of the Christian community are recalled in the words and actions of Jesus, in the feeding of the multitude, and in the gathering of the fragments so that the meal can continue. While Jesus has compassion on the lost sheep, without a shepherd (v 35), the disciples want Jesus to send them away. He commands them: 'You give them something to eat' (v 37). Out of the poverty of the disciples, Jesus generates a great meal, and enables them to nourish the five thousand who are gathered there.

The miracle is followed by *the first sea journey, and contrasting responses to Jesus* (6:45–56). The disciples do not recognise Jesus, who comes to them across the stormy seas, because their hearts are hardened and they have not understood about the loaves (vv 45–52). On arrival at Gennesaret, the opposite reaction takes place. Unlike the disciples, people 'recognized him' and he works many miracles (vv 53–56). But the life and practice of Jesus and his disciples generate *the first conflict* in the cycle, a conflict between Jesus and the traditions of Israel. In a bitter encounter, the Pharisees and the scribes attack Jesus on his lack of observance of purity traditions. He accuses them of rejecting the commandments of God and replacing them with human traditions (vv 1–13). He instructs 'the people' on the importance of what comes out of a person, rather than of what is eaten or touched from 'outside' and is superficial (vv 14–15). He further instructs his disciples on why this is so (vv 17–23). Much of the discussion surrounds the issue of food and eating, and this continues into *the first miraculous healings* in the cycle, two healings that take place in Gentile territory (7:24–37).

(see boxed text below)
In verse 24, Jesus walks out of Israel. In the region of Tyre and Sidon he meets a Syrophoenician woman (vv 25–26). Using a derogatory term, used by the Jews to speak of Gentiles, he challenges her to

---

Mark 7:24–37

24 From there he set out and went away to the region of Tyre. He entered a house and did not want anyone to know he was there. Yet he could not escape notice, 25 but a woman whose little daughter had an unclean spirit immediately heard about him, and she came and bowed down at his feet. 26 Now the woman was a Gentile, of Syrophoenician origin. She begged him to cast the demon out of her daughter. 27 He said to her, "Let the children be fed first, for it is not fair to take the children's food and throw it to the dogs." 28 But she answered him, "Sir, even the dogs under the table eat the children's crumbs." 29 Then he said to her, "For saying that, you may go—the demon has left your daughter." 30 So she went home, found the child lying on the bed, and the demon gone.

31 Then he returned from the region of Tyre, and went by way of Sidon towards the Sea of Galilee, in the region of the Decapolis. 32 They brought to him a deaf man who had an impediment in his speech; and they begged him to lay his hand on him. 33 He took him aside in private, away from the crowd, and put his fingers into his ears, and he spat and touched his tongue. 34 Then looking up to heaven, he sighed and said to him, "Ephphatha," that is, "Be opened." 35 And immediately his ears were opened, his tongue was released, and he spoke plainly. 36 Then Jesus ordered them to tell no one; but the more he ordered them, the more zealously they proclaimed it. 37 They were astounded beyond measure, saying, "He has done everything well; he even makes the deaf to hear and the mute to speak."

Mark 8:22–26

22 They came to Bethsaida. Some people brought a blind man to him and begged him to touch him. 23 He took the blind man by the hand and led him out of the village; and when he had put saliva on his eyes and laid his hands on him, he asked him, "Can you see anything?" 24 And the man looked up and said, "I can see people, but they look like trees, walking." 25 Then Jesus laid his hands on his eyes again; and he looked intently and his sight was restored, and he saw everything clearly. 26 Then he sent him away to his home, saying, "Do not even go into the village."

Mark 8:27–30

27 Jesus went on with his disciples to the villages of Caesarea Philippi; and on the way he asked his disciples, "Who do people say that I am?" 28 And they answered him, "John the Baptist; and others, Elijah; and still others, one of the prophets." 29 He asked them, "But who do you say that I am?" Peter answered him, "You are the Messiah." 30 And he sternly ordered them not to tell anyone about him.

---

recognise that she does not deserve to receive the gifts reserved for God's chosen people (v 27). She is open to this. She knows that she comes to him with empty hands, and with nothing to offer. It is precisely in her nothingness as a little dog under the table that she asks for the gift that only Jesus can give (v 28). In her nothingness she is blessed by the miracle (vv 24–30). An abundance of bread in the first bread miracle was given to the people of Israel. Their leaders have shown arrogance in 7:1–13. Jesus now shares his gift with a humble and open Gentile woman.

As Jesus moves from one place to another, by way of the Decapolis, he remains in a Gentile land (v 31). He cures a deaf mute not by using traditional miraculous methods, but by looking to the heavens and praying, in Aramaic, to God. As a result of this miracle, Gentiles become the first to suggest that Jesus might be the Messiah: 'He even makes the deaf to hear and the mute to speak' (v 37). Their words come from Isaiah 35:5–6, an accepted messianic text, suggesting that when the Messiah comes the deaf will hear and the dumb will speak (v 37). Gentiles use Israel's sacred Scriptures to proclaim a Messiah that Israel will not accept.

The second multiplication of the loaves and fish follows immediately (8:1–9). There are similarities and even parallels between the two bread miracles, especially concerning the Eucharistic nature of the meal, the responsibility of the disciples to feed the crowd of 'about four thousand people' and the gathering of the fragments at the end of the meal. The table remains open. But Jesus is in a Gentile land, on the other side of the lake. Other details in the narrative indicate that this feeding is a symbol of Jesus' ongoing Eucharistic presence to the Gentiles, for 'some of them have come from a great distance' (v 3). As Jesus has fed Israel, he now feeds the Gentile world. Following the miracle, Jesus dismisses the crowd, and sets out on *the second sea journey*, to Dalmanutha (8:10). Pharisees appear on the scene, and Jesus debates with them as *the second conflict* opens (8:11–13b). They ask for a sign from Jesus that will give authority to what he says and does, but he rejects their request, condemning them as 'this generation'. They are locked in a closed religious system that will allow no entry to the person and message of Jesus. The conflict with the Pharisees in verses 11 to 13b warns the disciples to be wary of the leaven of the Pharisees and the Herodians (v 15). But the disciples show they are moving dangerously close to that 'yeast' in their inability to recognise 'the bread' they have with them, and in their misunderstanding of the two bread miracles (vv 16–17). The disciples in the boat have become part of the *second conflict* in the cycle. Jesus asks them: '*Do you have eyes and fail to see?* Do you have ears and fail to hear?' (vv 18–19). He reminds them of his twofold abundant gift of bread (vv 20–21).

Blindness is central to *the second miraculous healing* (vv 22–26).

(See boxed text top left)

At Bethsaida, a blind man is cured, in stages. He moves from total blindness through partial sight to full vision. Mark first raises the theme of blindness in Jesus' accusation of the disciples in 8:18. It continues in the miracle of the man who gradually comes to full sight in verses 22 to 26. This is the strangest miracle in all of the Gospels. The man arrives completely blind (v 22). In a first moment, Jesus does actions that parallel other healings of people who were cured of eye problems — he makes spittle and puts it on the eyes. This generates

20 A Friendly Guide to Mark's Gospel

imperfect sight in the man (v 24). He sees men that look like trees walking. Only when Jesus takes the man aside and gazes at him, without any gestures, does the man see properly, and is dismissed from the scene (vv 25–26).

The confession at Caesarea Philippi (vv 27–30) needs to be read in the light of the story of the blind man.

(See boxed text bottom left)

The people who suggest that Jesus might be one of the precursors to the messianic era (John the Baptist, Elijah, one of the prophets) are totally blind to Jesus' identity (vv 27–28; see v 22). In response to Jesus' question, Peter's confession of the faith of the disciples, 'You are the Messiah', may appear to be a wonderful confession of faith — at last (see 1:1). But it may be partial sight (v 29; see v 24). To acclaim Jesus as the Messiah may mean that they are expecting *their* Messiah: an all-conquering hero who will come to restore Israel to its original Davidic kingdom. Thus, Peter is partially right, but in danger of getting it wrong. Thus, they are to say nothing. It could be misleading to proclaim Jesus' messianic status as Peter and the disciples understand it at this stage of the story (v 30). The rest of the Gospel story needs to be told for fullness of vision (matching the final experience of the blind man [v 25]). Jesus' words in verse 31 will open the second half of the story, and introduce that vision for the first time. Jesus is going to Jerusalem to suffer, to be slain and to rise again.

The confession at Caesarea Philippi is surely a moment of climax, but we should be careful not to separate one part of the story from another. Thus, as the first half of the Gospel comes to a close, the second half is already under way. The curing of a blind man at Bethsaida in 8:22–26 returns in the cure of blind Bartimaeus in 10:46–52. Between these two stories of blind men Jesus will three times tell of the forthcoming passion, death and resurrection of the Son of Man (8:31; 9:31; 10:32–34). This is a deliberate literary 'overlap' in which 8:22–30 concludes 1:14 – 8:30 and introduces 8:31 – 15:47.

DID YOU KNOW?

• Jesus is misunderstood and eventually abandoned by those closest to him

• 'Outsiders' express faith in Jesus — the Syrophoenician woman, Bartimaeus, Gentiles and lepers

• This belief of the outsiders is in contrast with the lack of faith of the disciples

• The progressive healing of the blind man (8:22–26) is not an indication of Jesus' lack of skill as a healer but of the journey in faith that must be taken from blindness to perfect vision

• The disciples were on this journey in faith and so are modern-day believers

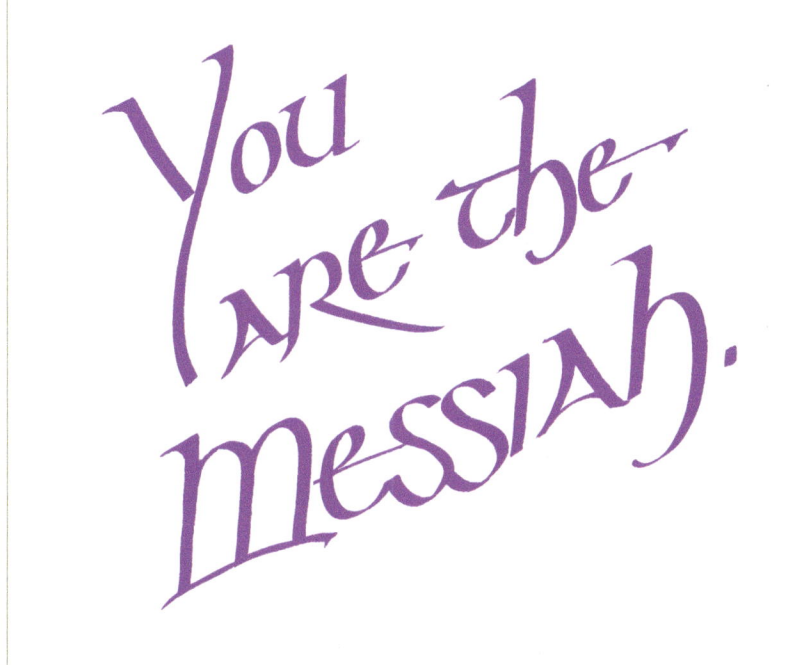

You are the Messiah.

The suffering and vindicated Son of Man: Christ and Son of God in Mark 8:31 – 15:47

1 — On the way from blindness to sight (8:31 – 10:52)

The miracle of the cure of the blind man at Bethsaida in Mark 8:22–26 returned to the theme of the blindness of the disciples, first raised by Jesus in 8:18, and opened a bridge passage (8:22–30) that led out of the first half of the story (1:1 – 8:30) into the second half (8:31 – 15:47). It points towards the second cure of a blind man, Bartimaeus, in 10:46–52. Between the two miracles, during which Jesus and the disciples are 'on the way' to Jerusalem, Jesus predicts his forthcoming passion (8:31, 9:31; 10:32–34). The first narrative unit (8:31 – 10:52) of the second half of the Gospel (8:31 – 15:47) begins with the first passion prediction of 8:31 and concludes with the second account of the curing of a blind man in 10:46–52. Jesus begins to teach his disciples that he, the Son of Man, must suffer, be rejected by the leaders of Israel, be killed and after three days rise (v 31).

(See boxed text right)
This is Jesus' *first prediction of his passion*. After Peter's confession that Jesus was the Christ, the disciples were warned not to say anything about this (vv 29–30), but Jesus proclaims his destiny as the

Mark 8:31–9:1

31 Then he began to teach them that the Son of Man must undergo great suffering, and be rejected by the elders, the chief priests, and the scribes, and be killed, and after three days rise again. 32 He said all this quite openly. And Peter took him aside and began to rebuke him.
33 But turning and looking at his disciples, he rebuked Peter and said, "Get behind me, Satan! For you are setting your mind not on divine things but on human things."

34 He called the crowd with his disciples, and said to them, "If any want to become my followers, let them deny themselves and take up their cross and follow me. 35 For those who want to save their life will lose it, and those who lose their life for my sake, and for the sake of the gospel, will save it. 36 For what will it profit them to gain the whole world and forfeit their life? 37 Indeed, what can they give in return for their life? 38 Those who are ashamed of me and of my words in this adulterous and sinful generation, of them the Son of Man will also be ashamed when he comes in the glory of his Father with the holy angels."

9 And he said to them, "Truly I tell you, there are some standing here who will not taste death until they see that the Kingdom of God has come with power."

suffering Son of Man 'quite openly' (v 32). This is the answer to the 'mystery' of the person of Jesus, the theme of 1:14 – 8:30. But Peter refuses to accept Jesus' words, takes hold of Jesus and rebukes him (v 32). Jesus' sharp reply to Peter indicates he has *failed to understand and to accept the destiny of Jesus*. Disciples were called 'to follow' Jesus (see 1:16–20), but Peter is blocking his way, as he heads towards Jerusalem. For this he is Satan, a stumbling block, and must take his place as a disciple — behind Jesus (v 33). But Jesus does not abandon his disciples. *He calls them and the crowd and instructs them* on the need to take up their cross, to lose their lives for the sake of the Gospel (v 34). In this way they will save their lives, made available in and through Jesus (vv 35–36). There is a mutuality that must be established between the disciple and Jesus. Whoever refuses Jesus, will be refused by Jesus, and whoever accepts him will be welcomed by him when the Son of Man returns in glory (vv 37–38). They will join Jesus in the glory he will attain by means of his death and resurrection (9:1). The destiny of Jesus is to be the destiny of the disciple.

A pattern is emerging: the passion prediction is followed by failure on the part of the disciples, yet Jesus does not abandon them in their failure. He calls them and instructs them further on the nature of true discipleship.

The transfiguration (9:2–8) reveals to Peter, James and John that Jesus is the Son of God. The disciples, who have been told of the need to take up their own cross (8:34) and have heard Jesus' telling of his future suffering and death in Jerusalem, are instructed that they must listen to him, as he is the beloved Son of God (v 7). The three disciples are full of fear, and yet want to hold on to that moment on the mountain, to build three tents (vv 5–6). This is to fail to accept that Jesus' destiny lies in Jerusalem, not enfolded in glory in a tent. The vision fades, and only Jesus remains (v 8). Leading them down the mountain, he teaches them further about the need for the Son of Man to suffer, just as John the Baptist suffered (vv 9–13). The disciples expected the prophet Elijah to return before the time of the Son of Man, but Jesus tells them he has come in the person of John the Baptist. They must not share this information until Jesus has risen from the dead. They do not understand what 'rising from the dead' might mean (v 10).

The disciples continue to fail in the next episode (vv 14–29), unable to understand why — by their own authority — they cannot cure the epileptic boy (vv 18, 28). In a context highlighted by the faith and trust of the boy's father (v 24), Jesus has a moment of exasperation as he speaks to his disciples: 'You faithless generation, how much longer must

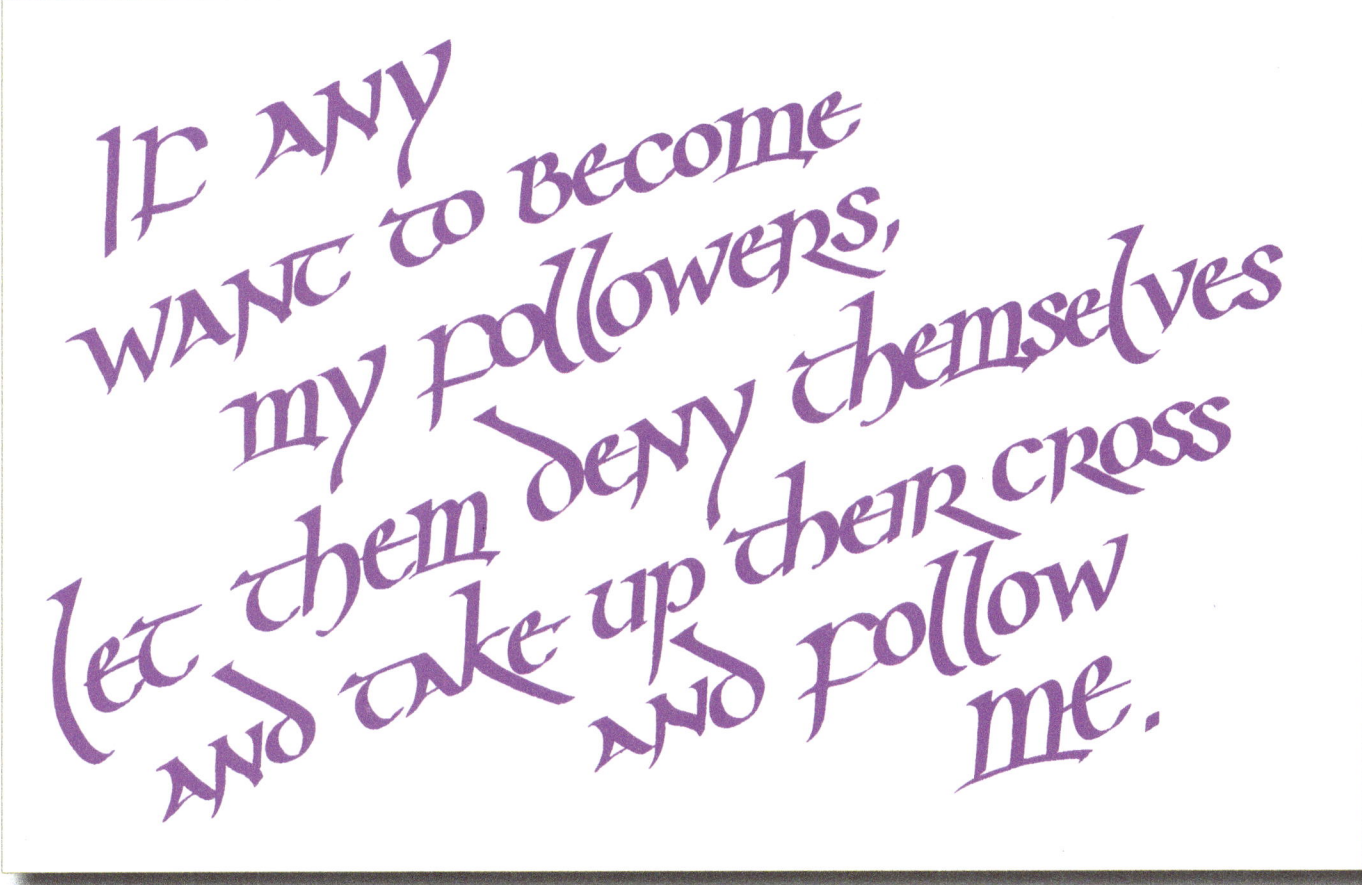

If any want to become my followers, let them deny themselves and take up their cross and follow me.

A FRIENDLY GUIDE TO MARK'S GOSPEL 23

Mark 10:2–31

2 Some Pharisees came, and to test him they asked, "Is it lawful for a man to divorce his wife?" 3 He answered them, "What did Moses command you?" 4 They said, "Moses allowed a man to write a certificate of dismissal and to divorce her." 5 But Jesus said to them, "Because of your hardness of heart he wrote this commandment for you. 6 But from the beginning of creation, 'God made them male and female.' 7 'For this reason a man shall leave his father and mother and be joined to his wife, 8 and the two shall become one flesh.' So they are no longer two, but one flesh. 9 Therefore what God has joined together, let no one separate."

10 Then in the house the disciples asked him again about this matter. 11 He said to them, "Whoever divorces his wife and marries another commits adultery against her; 12 and if she divorces her husband and marries another, she commits adultery."

13 People were bringing little children to him in order that he might touch them; and the disciples spoke sternly to them. 14 But when Jesus saw this, he was indignant and said to them, "Let the little children come to me; do not stop them; for it is to such as these that the Kingdom of God belongs. 15 Truly I tell you, whoever does not receive the Kingdom of God as a little child will never enter it." 16 And he took them up in his arms, laid his hands on them, and blessed them.

17 As he was setting out on a journey, a man ran up and knelt before him, and asked him, "Good Teacher, what must I do to inherit eternal life?" 18 Jesus said to him, "Why do you call me good? No one is good but God alone. 19 You know the commandments: 'You shall not murder; You shall not commit adultery; You shall not steal; You shall not bear false witness; You shall not defraud; Honor your father and mother.' " 20 He said to him, "Teacher, I have kept all these since my youth." 21 Jesus, looking at him, loved him and said, "You lack one thing; go, sell what you own, and give the money to the poor, and you will have treasure in heaven; then come, follow me." 22 When he heard this, he was shocked and went away grieving, for he had many possessions.

23 Then Jesus looked around and said to his disciples, "How hard it will be for those who have wealth to enter the Kingdom of God!" 24 And the disciples were perplexed at these words. But Jesus said to them again, "Children, how hard it is to enter the Kingdom of God! 25 It is easier for a camel to go through the eye of a needle than for someone who is rich to enter the Kingdom of God." 26 They were greatly astounded and said to one another, "Then who can be saved?" 27 Jesus looked at them and said, "For mortals it is impossible, but not for God; for God all things are possible."

28 Peter began to say to him, "Look, we have left everything and followed you." 29 Jesus said, "Truly I tell you, there is no one who has left house or brothers or sisters or mother or father or children or fields, for my sake and for the sake of the good news, 30 who will not receive a hundredfold now in this age—houses, brothers and sisters, mothers and children, and fields, with persecutions—and in the age to come eternal life. 31 But many who are first will be last, and the last will be first."

I be among you? How much longer must I put up with you?' (v 19). Yet he takes them aside and instructs them that authority to work such marvels has its source in God: 'This kind can come out only through prayer' (v 29).

Jesus continues the journey with the disciples. He is teaching them, by means of *the second prediction of the passion*: 'The Son of Man is to be betrayed into human hands, and they will kill him' (vv 30–31). This is followed by the *second failure of the disciples to understand and to accept* the destiny of Jesus. They did not understand, as they were discussing who was the greatest (vv 33–34). Jesus *instructs his failing disciples* on their call to be the servants of all and last of all, and on the receptivity of a true disciple by means of the receptivity of a small child (vv 35–37). But still the disciples fail. John reports that they forbade someone from casting out demons in the name of Jesus, because that person was *not following them*. Jesus insists that the reigning presence of God is made manifest in those who do things in his name, not by those who are following the disciples (vv 38–41). One must follow Jesus, not the disciples.

A series of warnings by Jesus follows, further instructing the disciples on the seriousness of their responsibilities as receptive servants, and not lords. The kingdom is more precious than any part of one's body (vv 42–48), and salt that has lost its saltiness has lost its worth (v 49). You can survive without a hand, a foot or an eye. You have two of them. But to lose the kingdom is to lose everything that is precious. The disciples must put first things first; they must be full of the qualities that mark people as being disciples of Jesus. The meaning of Jesus' words across this section is caught in his final comment: 'be at peace with one another' (v 50).

Jesus' instruction of the disciples has focused upon three major themes: the call to take up the cross (8:34 – 9:1), the need for service and the need for receptivity (9:32–37). In 10:1–30 these demands continue, but no longer at the level of theory. (see boxed text left)

In 10:1–12, by means of a debate with the Pharisees who wish to test him (v 2), his opponents find in Moses' teaching permission for a man to divorce one's wife (v 3). Jesus explains that God's original design was that one man cleave to a lifelong bond with one woman, and that Moses allowed divorce because of 'your hardness of heart' (vv 4–9). The reader and listener have learnt in the prologue that in Jesus and his teaching, God's original design has been restored (see 1:1, 10, 13). The disciples find this a difficult teaching, so he gathers them in the house, and reaffirms it (vv 10–11). The focus on the disciples must be noticed. It is not enough to teach the *theory* of the cross and receptivity. The teachings must be acted out in the intimacy of *one's life* as a disciple. In a brief interlude, the theme of the receptivity of the disciple is restated, as Jesus again takes children in his arms and blesses them, as the disciples object (vv 13–16).

This episode is followed by the story of the man who wishes to inherit eternal life (vv 17–18). He is called by Jesus to reach beyond the observance of the social commandments of the Law, to give up his riches so that he might become one of his followers (vv 19–20). The man cannot make this step, despite the love that Jesus has for him (v 21). He walks away, a lost vocation to discipleship (v 22). Again Jesus turns to the disciples, and this time he speaks to them about riches, insisting that 'It is easier for a camel to go through the eye of a needle than for someone who is rich to enter the Kingdom of God' (v 25). But this is impossible! Looking back across Jesus' teaching on divorce, and now his teaching on possession, the disciples ask: 'Then who can be saved?' (v 26). Jesus appears to be asking the impossible, but for the disciple who is receptive to the action of God, everything is possible: 'For mortals it is impossible, but not for God; for God all things are possible' (v 27).

Peter's awareness that the disciples have made such sacrifices enables Jesus to praise them, and promise them a hundredfold, both now and hereafter (vv 29–31). Serving and receptive disciples are called to follow Jesus' way, through death, to life and the kingdom that only God can give. But the practice of receptivity and the taking up of one's cross is now firmly anchored in the practicalities of the disciples' lives: their affections (vv 2–12) and their possessions (vv 17–27).

The journey of Jesus and his disciples to Jerusalem continues, as Jesus strides ahead and his followers are full of fear and amazement (10:32). In that situation, Jesus utters *the third passion prediction*, replete with the details of his suffering and passion (vv 33–34). There can be no misunderstanding of the full implications of this final prediction, but James and John do. They ask for positions on the right and on the left of Jesus when he comes to his glory in Jerusalem (v 35). They seek positions of power and authority in the messianic kingdom that Peter dreamt of in his confession of 8:29 (vv 36–37). *The third failure of the disciples to understand and accept* the destiny of Jesus is again met by a patient Jesus. He promises them a share in his sufferings, and tells them that a position on the right or the left is not his to give (vv 38–39). When Jesus comes to Jerusalem, criminals will hang on his right and his left (see 15:27).

Mark 10:46–52

46 They came to Jericho. As he and his disciples and a large crowd were leaving Jericho, Bartimaeus son of Timaeus, a blind beggar, was sitting by the roadside. 47 When he heard that it was Jesus of Nazareth, he began to shout out and say, "Jesus, Son of David, have mercy on me!" 48 Many sternly ordered him to be quiet, but he cried out even more loudly, "Son of David, have mercy on me!" 49 Jesus stood still and said, "Call him here." And they called the blind man, saying to him, "Take heart; get up, he is calling you." 50 So throwing off his cloak, he sprang up and came to Jesus. 51 Then Jesus said to him, "What do you want me to do for you?" The blind man said to him, "My teacher, let me see again." 52 Jesus said to him, "Go; your faith has made you well." Immediately he regained his sight and followed him on the way.

This third failure is compounded by the indignation of the other members of the Twelve, annoyed that James and John are jockeying for positions of power (v 41). Jesus turns to them, and continues *to instruct his failing disciples*. Jesus insists that they are not to imitate accepted patterns of so-called greatness: 'whoever wishes to become great among you must be your servant, and whoever wishes to be first among you must be slave of all' (vv 43–44). Jesus' final words to the disciples bring to a close all he has said to them by pointing to his own mission. Jesus is the model for the disciple. His disciples are to accept the cross (see 8:34 – 9:1), to be receptive servants (see 9:33–37). However, he does not ask it of his followers as a distant law-maker. He invites them to follow him: 'For the Son of Man came not to be served but to serve, and to give his life a ransom for many' (v 45).

The disciples, as they have been presented by Mark across 8:31 – 10:45, have never reached the third stage of total sight, promised by the gradual movement from blindness to imperfect sight to full sight in the cure of the blind man at Bethsaida (8:22–26). They are not prepared to abandon all and follow the suffering Son of Man to Jerusalem. Jesus' curing of the blind Bartimaeus (10:46–52) shows that such self-abandonment is possible.

(see boxed text on page 25)
Jesus is journeying along the road to Jerusalem, as he comes out from Jericho *with his disciples* and a large crowd of people (v 46a). Blind Bartimaeus is stationary, sitting at the side of the road (v 46b). Jesus hears the blind man shouting out to him in trust and faith (vv 47–49) and stops. He asks the onlookers to 'call' Bartimaeus to come over to him (see v 49, where the verb 'to call' appears three times). Motion restarts: Bartimaeus leaps to his feet, leaving behind his cloak, his only possession. He comes to Jesus with nothing but himself, like the Syrophoenician woman, ready to receive whatever Jesus will offer. In response to his request, Jesus tells him that his faith has made him well, and invites him to go on his way (vv 50–51). The way of Bartimaeus is Jesus' journey. He follows Jesus down *his* way (v 52). The story of Bartimaeus stands in contrast to the preceding failure of the disciples and symbolises the ability of those who have faith in Jesus to see the truth. It also brings to a close the journey from one blind miracle (8:22–26) to another (10:46–52).

Whoever wishes to become great among you must be your servant, and whoever wishes to be first among you must be a slave of all.

II — Endings in Jerusalem (11:1 – 13:37)

Jesus' words and deeds in 11:1 – 13:37 bring significant Jewish institutions to an end, and forecast the destruction of Jerusalem and the end of the world. Jesus halts Israel's cultic practices in the Temple (11:1–25). He then systematically challenges and reduces to silence the religious leaders of Israel: Sadducees, Pharisees and scribes (11:27 – 12:24). Finally, sitting on the Mount of Olives, looking across the valley towards the splendour of Jerusalem and its Temple (13:1–2), he foretells the destruction of the Holy City (13:3–23) and the end of the world (13:24–37).

The end of Israel's cult (11:1–25)

On arrival at villages that lie on the outskirts of the great city, Jesus prepares to enter Jerusalem (v 1). He tells two of his disciples where they are to go, what they will find, and what they must say and do (vv 2–3). It happens exactly as Jesus said (vv 4–6), and the stage is set for Jesus' entry, riding the colt brought by the disciples. Jesus is lavishly welcomed as he approaches the city (vv 7–8). The spreading of garments and laying of leafy branches accompany a cry *from those who followed and those who went before* that welcomes Jesus as the Messiah: 'Hosanna! Blessed is the one who comes in the name of the Lord! Blessed is the coming kingdom of our ancestor David! Hosanna in the highest' (vv 9–10). These words go no further than the confession of Peter in 8:29, and the false expectation of the disciples from 8:31 – 10:45. It is 'those who followed' who utter this cry,

Mark 11:12–25

12 On the following day, when they came from Bethany, he was hungry. 13 Seeing in the distance a fig tree in leaf, he went to see whether perhaps he would find anything on it. When he came to it, he found nothing but leaves, for it was not the season for figs. 14 He said to it, "May no one ever eat fruit from you again." And his disciples heard it.

15 Then they came to Jerusalem. And he entered the temple and began to drive out those who were selling and those who were buying in the temple, and he overturned the tables of the money changers and the seats of those who sold doves; 16 and he would not allow anyone to carry anything through the temple. 17 He was teaching and saying, "Is it not written,

'My house shall be called a house of prayer for all the nations'?
But you have made it a den of robbers."

18 And when the chief priests and the scribes heard it, they kept looking for a way to kill him; for they were afraid of him, because the whole crowd was spellbound by his teaching. 19 And when evening came, Jesus and his disciples went out of the city.

20 In the morning as they passed by, they saw the fig tree withered away to its roots. 21 Then Peter remembered and said to him, "Rabbi, look! The fig tree that you cursed has withered." 22 Jesus answered them, "Have faith in God. 23 Truly I tell you, if you say to this mountain, 'Be taken up and thrown into the sea,' and if you do not doubt in your heart, but believe that what you say will come to pass, it will be done for you. 24 So I tell you, whatever you ask for in prayer, believe that you have received it, and it will be yours.

25 "Whenever you stand praying, forgive, if you have anything against anyone; so that your Father in heaven may also forgive you your trespasses."

DID YOU KNOW?

- Mark presents Jesus as an active healer and miracle worker — a man of action

- But Jesus also accepts loneliness and suffering as the cost of obedience to God's will

- Mark's Gospel narrative makes two basic theological affirmations:
  ≈ Jesus is the Christ, the Son of Man and the Son of God
  ≈ those who would be disciples must take up their own cross and follow him

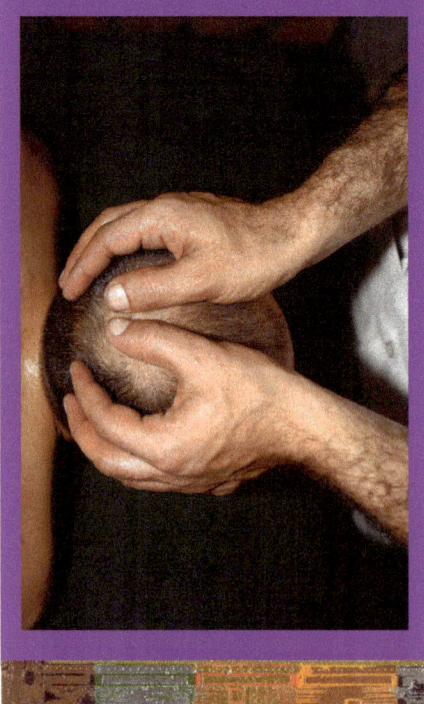

the disciples of Jesus who continue to misread Jesus' messianic program (v 9). He has not come to bring the Kingdom of David, but the Kingdom of God. Only after this false acclamation does Jesus enter Jerusalem, go to the Temple and look around at everything (v 11). There is something ominous about this survey of the Temple, and his anger will burst forth in the next scene. For the moment, he leaves the city and goes to Bethany.

Another 'sandwich construction' reappears. On the way from Bethany to Jerusalem, Jesus sees the fig tree in leaf, seeks its fruit and curses it.

(see boxed text on page 27)

The fig tree is cursed because it was not the 'proper time' (Greek: *kairos*; NRSV: 'the season') for fruit (vv 12–14). Why curse the fig tree on these grounds? The answer will be provided during and after the next episode (vv 15–25). Jesus brings to an end the money dealings that went on at the entry to the Temple: buying, selling and money changing (v 15). But these deals were essential to the cultic activity of the Temple. People who carried coins with effigies had to exchange them for coins bearing no image in order to respect the holiness of the place they were entering, and the pigeons were the sacrificial victims used by the very poor. In a translation not found in most Bibles, Mark in fact next reports: 'and he would not allow anyone to carry any *sacred vessel* (Greek: *skeuos*) through the temple' (v 16). This translation catches the meaning of the episode (NRSV: 'to carry anything' misses it). Jesus brings to an end all the cultic activity in the Temple. His house is to be a house of prayer for all the nations. It has been reduced to a den of robbers. The next day, as Jesus and the disciples

again return to Jerusalem, Peter notices that the fig tree has died and withered (vv 20–21). The fig tree is a symbol of an Israel that did not recognise its 'proper time' (NRSV: 'season') and thus has lost its life-giving authority, and has withered. In response to Peter's amazement that the fig tree has withered (see v 21), Jesus teaches his disciples that his coming, his presence among them and his teaching (and implicitly his death and resurrection) create a new way to God (v 23). The cult of Israel may have been symbolically brought to a standstill in 11:12–21, but in its place, Jesus insists: 'Have faith in God' (v 22), and teaches his disciples the power of such faith (v 23). He further instructs them: 'whatever you ask for in prayer, believe that you have received it, and it will be yours' (v 24), and finally, lest prayer become mere words, not reflected in action, he adds, 'Whenever you stand praying, forgive' (v 25). In place of the cultic practices of Israel, Jesus teaches the way of faith, prayer and forgiveness. In this way, the disciple of Jesus turns to God, and God turns towards the believer.

THE END OF ISRAEL'S RELIGIOUS LEADERSHIP (11:27 – 12:44)

Jesus is challenged by a collection of people from the Jewish leadership: the chief priests, the scribes and the elders (v 27). They demand an explanation of his authority (v 28). He outwits them by responding with a question of his own. He asks whether the baptism of John was from heaven or from men (v 29). Given the popularity of John the Baptist (see vv 30–32), they remain silent, and thus this first encounter results in a stalemate, neither party responding to the questions posed (v 33). This leads Jesus to speak to the leaders 'in parables' (12:1).

The parable of 12:1–12 is loosely based upon the image of a vineyard to speak of Israel in Isaiah 5:1–2. The central message of the parable concerns a lord and master who had given tenants the privilege of caring for his vineyard, and tenants who do not live out their role in loyalty to the master. They wish to inherit the vineyard itself, beat and insult all the servants who come from him, and in the end kill his beloved son, and cast him out of the vineyard (vv 2–8). The response of the master is rapid: the tenants are destroyed and the vineyard given to others, a strong reference to the destruction of Jerusalem. The story of Jesus, who proclaims and lives the reigning presence of God, only to be rejected and slain by those whom God had entrusted with the care of Israel, is the message of the parable. Jesus also reminds them of the Word of God, found in Psalm 118:22–23: 'The stone that the builders rejected has become the chief cornerstone.

This is the Lord's doing; it is marvelous in our eyes' (see vv 10–11). During the story of Jesus' passion and death, the suggestion that the rejected Jesus will become the foundation stone of a new Temple returns with force. The leaders of Israel slink off in silence: 'they realized that he had told this parable against them' (v 12).

Three encounters with the key groups in that leadership follow. The Pharisees and the Herodians, who had plotted in 3:6 to destroy Jesus, challenge him. Attempting to trap him by placing him in an impossible position: they ask whether or not taxes should be paid to Caesar (vv 13–15a). If he says 'yes', they can accuse him of disloyalty to Israel (which would make him objectionable to the Pharisees). If he says 'no', he can be regarded as a revolutionary (which would be objectionable to the Herodians). He says neither, but asks his questioners to provide a coin (v 15). They do so, and give him a coin bearing the effigy of Caesar (v 16). *But they are in the Temple (see 11:27), and should not be carrying coins bearing effigies (see 11:15).* It is on this basis that Jesus can utter his famous words, which have the immediate purpose of showing the duplicity of his questioners, but which have rightly taken on a broader meaning over the centuries:

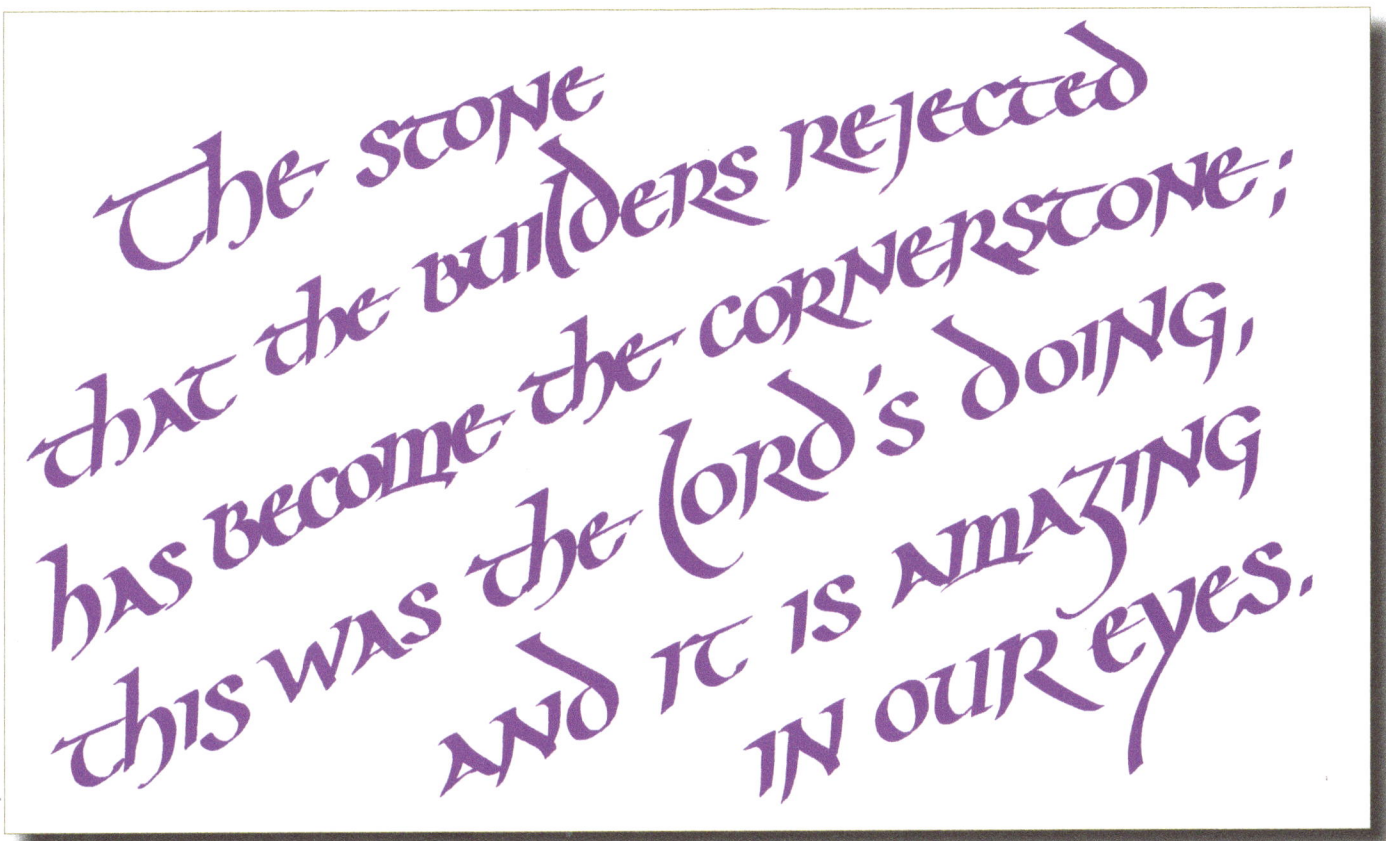

The stone that the builders rejected has become the cornerstone; this was the Lord's doing, and it is amazing in our eyes.

A FRIENDLY GUIDE TO MARK'S GOSPEL 29

'Give to the emperor the things that are the emperor's, and to God the things that are God's' (12:17a). They are reduced to silent amazement (v 17b).

The Sadducees only accept the Books of Moses (the Torah) as the revealed Word of God and thus do not believe in the resurrection of the dead. They step forward to challenge Jesus (v 18). They also test Jesus' loyalty to the word of Moses, citing the case of a childless woman who has married all seven brothers of a family, at the death of each husband, as she should. To whom is she the wife in the resurrection (vv 19–23)? Jesus responds to them by charging them with ignorance of the Scriptures and the power of God (v 24). He first explains the power of God, indicating that life after the resurrection will be a complete transformation of human experience. Their question reflects a misunderstanding of the transforming power of God who raises people from their tombs (v 25). He then turns to a text from Moses (Ex 3:6), taken from the famous episode of Moses' encounter with God at the burning bush (Ex 3:1–22). When speaking to Moses, God is identified as the God of the Patriarchs: Abraham, Isaac and Jacob. The Word of God, who must be a God of the living, affirms that the Patriarchs, long since dead as God speaks to Moses, must somehow be alive in the resurrection (vv 26–27a). Not only do the Sadducees not understand the transforming power of God, but they do not understand the Scriptures that came to them from Moses (v 24). Jesus closes his encounter with the Sadducees by bluntly declaring: 'you are quite wrong' (v 27b).

The next figure to enter the story is a scribe (v 28a) who asks Jesus' opinion concerning the first of all the commandments (v 28b). Jesus responds by citing Deuteronomy 6:5, on the need to love God above all things, with one's heart, soul, mind and strength, and adding a further citation from Leviticus 19:18, indicating that one must also love one's neighbour as oneself (vv 29–31). The scribe accepts this teaching, and agrees with Jesus that these commandments exceed all the burnt offerings and cultic sacrifices (vv 32–33). Jesus applauds *this scribe*, and tells

him he is close to the Kingdom of God. It is Jesus' word that utters the truth and the scribe accepts it. The series of encounters in the Temple between Jesus and the chief priests, the scribes and the elders (11:27 – 12:12); the Pharisees and the Herodians (12:13–17); the Sadducees (vv 17–27); and a scribe (vv 28–34) comes to a close with a comment from Mark: 'After that no one dared to ask him any question' (v 34). Jesus has reduced the religious authorities of Israel to silence.

However, Jesus' encounters with the scribal traditions of Israel have not come to an end. As he teaches in the Temple, he questions the scribes' teaching that the Christ is the Son of David (v 35). By means of an exegesis of Psalm 110:1, Jesus points out that David, inspired by the Holy Spirit, speaks of the Lord, who addresses the Messiah whom David calls 'my Lord', and who commands the Messiah to sit at his right hand (v 36). The Spirit-filled David thus speaks of the Messiah as 'my Lord'. It is impossible, therefore, that the Messiah, who is David's Lord, can be his son (v 37a). In contrast to the silence generated by the earlier encounters with the leadership of Israel, this teaching meets with great approval from the crowd (v 37b).

The theme of 'widows' locks together Mark's closing presentation of Jesus' encounter with the religious leaders of Israel. As Jesus teaches, he warns against the superficiality of the scribes who like to wear long robes, be saluted in the marketplace and have the best seats at celebrations (vv 38–39). These gestures hide evil men who publicly make long prayers, 'for the sake of appearances', but privately exploit the poor and suffering, as they 'devour widows' houses' (v 40ab). They are promised condemnation (v 40c). The scene changes, but a widow reappears. Jesus and his disciples watch the wealthy put large sums of money into the treasury (v 41). A poor widow puts in the two copper coins that made up a penny (v 42). Turning to his disciples, Jesus, who has brought the leaders of Israel to silence and condemned false religion, points to her as the model of a disciple. While many give out of their abundance, and thus lose nothing in their gift, the woman gives her all. The Greek word used (*bios*), placed emphatically at the very end of the sentence and the passage as a whole, speaks of what the woman gives. It has two meanings: the woman has put in 'all she had to live on' (*bios*), and thus has given all her possessions, but she has also given her very life (*bios*).

Symbolically, Jesus has brought to an end the leadership of Israel. Earlier in his encounter with the leaders of Israel, Jesus had promised a new Temple would arise on the cornerstone rejected by the builders (12:10–11). After the death and resurrection of Jesus, the disciples will be part of this new Temple (see 14:28; 16:7). They are instructed in this closing scene to give their all, their very lives (vv 43–44).

The end of Jerusalem (13:1–23) and the end of the world (vv 24–37)

Jesus' ministry closes with a solemn discourse, delivered on the Mount of Olives, looking across the valley towards Jerusalem and its Temple. Coming out of the Temple, the disciples admire its wonder, and Jesus tells them that soon all will be destroyed. He then sits down with them on the Mount of Olives, and Peter, James, John and Andrew, the first disciples to be called (1:16–20), ask two questions: when will this be and what will be the sign of its final accomplishment? These questions set the agenda for the discourse. In verses 5 to 23 Jesus will answer the first question, telling them of the end of Jerusalem and its Temple. In verses 24 to 37 he will speak of the end of the world. Mark has carefully arranged Jesus' teaching on the end of Jerusalem, focusing upon the experiences of the city and its people, and the need to recognise that the disaster of the destruction of Jerusalem by Titus and the Roman armies in AD 70 was not the end of the world. First, the Gospel had to be preached to all the nations (v 10).

False prophets (vv 5–6) Jesus warns the disciples against those who will arise among them, and claim that the return of the Messiah is taking place. They will claim, 'I am he!' and they will lead many astray. This must be prevented.

Wars and rumours of wars (vv 7–8) The readers of the Gospel hear of wars and rumours of wars, as reports of the tragic events of Jerusalem come to their ears. But this must not be understood as the end of time. There will be many wars, earthquakes and famines between now and the end of time. This is but the beginning.

Preach the Gospel to all nations (vv 9–13) A long experience of trial and suffering, at the hands and in the courts of both Jews and Gentiles, lies ahead of the readers of the Gospel. They must not fear betrayal and death, as they will be guided by the Spirit, and those who endure to the end will be saved. All this is necessary because before the end of the world 'the good news must first be proclaimed to all nations' (v 10).

Wars and rumours of wars (vv 14–20) Jesus now describes for the disciples events that can be reconstructed from existing reports about the Jewish War: Titus and his standard bearers

You shall love your neighbour as yourself.

in the Holy of Holies (v 14: the abomination of desolation that the reader must understand), the need to flee in haste, and the tribulations for mothers and those with child, as they flee into a beginning wintertime. They will survive only because of God's care for those he has called.

False prophets (vv 21–23) Jesus again warns the disciples against any acceptance of the many voices who may be crying out that this is the end of time. They have now been told that first the Gospel must be preached to all nations (v 10). False prophets will come and go, as will wars and rumours of wars. None of this should shake them in their mission as Jesus comforts them: 'I have already told you everything' (v 23).

The disasters surrounding the fall of Jerusalem and the destruction of the Temple do not mark the end of time and the final coming of the Son of Man as judge. However, that time will come, and all readers of the Gospel must watch and wait. Making a clear break from what he has said about the end of Jerusalem in verses 5 to 23, in verse 24, Jesus changes his focus by means of a strong adversative 'but'.

Jesus gathers images from the Old Testament to speak of the final end of time: darkness over the earth, the falling of the stars and the shaking of the heavenly powers (see Isa 13:10; Joel 2:10; 3:4; 3:15; Isa 34:4). At the end of all time the Son of Man will come in the clouds with power and glory. The suffering Son of Man, to whom authority has been given over the Sabbath and to forgive sins (see 2:10, 28), but whose authority is always questioned or rejected, will come as the final judge. He will send out angels, to gather the elect from the four corners of the earth. Jesus has told the disciples that the Gospel must first be preached to all the nations (v 10). Only when that has been done will the Son of Man be able to gather the elect 'from the four winds, from the ends of the earth to the ends of heaven' (v 27). Universal mission necessarily precedes the final coming of the Son of Man.

The signs given in verses 24 to 27 had to be read and understood, just as anyone who sees the sprouting of the fig tree must know that the summer is coming (v 28). There can be no doubt that everything will change and the world as the disciples know it will come to an end. That end will be very soon (v 30). However, one thing will remain, and the disciples who have been with Jesus, as well as disciples to whom this Gospel is addressed, must take comfort: 'Heaven and earth will pass away, but my words will not pass away' (v 31).

The exact time of the end remains, as in the Old Testament, the day *of the Lord*. No one knows when it will be: not the angels in heaven, not even the Son, and certainly not the disciples (vv 32–33). Jesus' tone changes. He no longer tells them of the events that are coming, nor does he continue to warn that they should take heed. He has used a warning verb (Greek: *blepô*) throughout the discourse (see vv 5, 9, 23, 33). From now on he insists that the disciples 'watch' (Greek: *grêgoreô*); warning becomes exhortation. The new verb insists that disciples act in a way that shows a preparedness to accept one's responsibilities. They are 'to be on the watch' as a good doorkeeper must do as his master leaves (v 34). This final part of the discourse, therefore, suggests that Jesus is about to leave the disciples, and that they must perform their task in his absence with diligence and care. We know that Jesus' departure will be through the cross. The disciples should also know, as on three occasions Jesus has told them of his imminent death and resurrection in Jerusalem (8:31; 9:31; 10:33–34). Thus, Jesus' final warnings and recommendations to his disciples look forward to and match the time periods that mark his passion and death in chapters 14 and 15. The disciples are told that they do not know whether the master of the house will come in the evening (see 14:17: arrest and betrayal), at midnight (see 14:32–65: Jewish hearing), at cockcrow (see 14:72: denials) or in the morning (see 15:1: Roman trial and crucifixion). He will come suddenly and find them asleep (see 14:32–42). The fragile first disciples hear Jesus' words as he enters into his passion: 'what I say to you I say to all: Keep awake' (v 37).

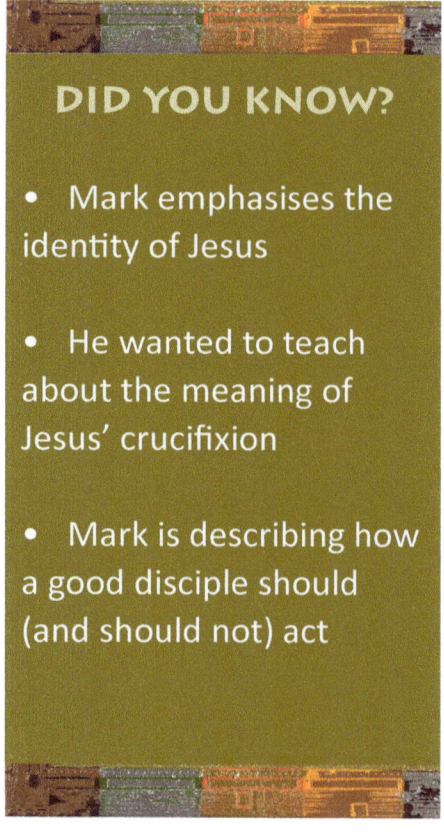

DID YOU KNOW?

- Mark emphasises the identity of Jesus

- He wanted to teach about the meaning of Jesus' crucifixion

- Mark is describing how a good disciple should (and should not) act

The Passion of Jesus: Mark 14:1 – 15:47

Jesus of Nazareth, whom his followers believed was the Christ, had been ignominiously crucified. As Paul confesses: 'We proclaim Christ crucified, a stumbling block to Jews and foolishness to Gentiles' (1 Cor 1:23). Mark's passion story shows us that the crucified Jesus was the Christ, the Son of God, in whom the Father was well pleased (see 1:1, 11).

Jewish trial: Jesus, the disciples and the leaders of Israel (14:1–72)

Mark's use of the 'sandwich construction' reappears. But in 14:1–72 it extends over eleven scenes. For the purposes of what follows, scenes marked (A) tell of the steady progress of the plot against Jesus, and the disciples' association with it. Scenes marked (B) highlight Jesus' role. The eleven scenes indicate moments of darkness and light. Together they form a powerful story that flows dramatically from one event to the other.

(A) Mark sets the story of Jesus' passion two days before the celebration of the Passover, the Feast of the Unleavened Bread (v 14a). The chief priests and scribes hatch a plan to slay Jesus, but fear an uprising from the people, who have so enthusiastically welcomed Jesus (see 11:1–11).

(B) The nameless woman of verses 3 to 9 who anoints Jesus also steps forward as a moment of light in the increasing darkness. In her unconditional self-gift to Jesus, symbolised by the smashing of the precious flask, and the pouring out of the oil, the theme of Jesus' royal status (v 3) is broached. The disciples are unhappy with such generosity, reproach her and miss the meaning of the gesture (vv 4–5). Jesus corrects them, saying that she has anointed his body for burial, and that 'wherever the good news is proclaimed in the whole world, what she has done will be told in remembrance of her' (v 9). The story is itself a proclamation of good news and repeats the self-gift of the widow of 12:41–44.

(A) The darkness deepens, as 'one of the twelve' turns against Jesus. In 3:14 Jesus appointed Judas to the Twelve. But in 3:19, Mark informed the readers that he would 'betray him'. The process begins here (v 10) as the promise of money (v 11) links Judas with a plot to kill Jesus. The process that began in stealth (vv 1–2) now becomes possible.

(B) Mark brings Jesus back to the centre of the action, accepting God's will, arranging for the events that follow. As the Passover is at hand, the disciples ask Jesus about the preparation for the meal (v 12). He gives them a series of commands (vv 13–15). What he

A Friendly Guide to Mark's Gospel 33

Mark 14:17–31

17 When it was evening, he came with the twelve. 18 And when they had taken their places and were eating, Jesus said, "Truly I tell you, one of you will betray me, one who is eating with me." 19 They began to be distressed and to say to him one after another, "Surely, not I?" 20 He said to them, "It is one of the twelve, one who is dipping bread into the bowl with me. 21 For the Son of Man goes as it is written of him, but woe to that one by whom the Son of Man is betrayed! It would have been better for that one not to have been born."

22 While they were eating, he took a loaf of bread, and after blessing it he broke it, gave it to them, and said, "Take; this is my body." 23 Then he took a cup, and after giving thanks he gave it to them, and all of them drank from it. 24 He said to them, "This is my blood of the covenant, which is poured out for many. 25 Truly I tell you, I will never again drink of the fruit of the vine until that day when I drink it new in the Kingdom of God."
(continued on page 35)

says will happen, does happen. Preparations are on the way for the meal that soon follows (v 16). Despite what lies ahead, Jesus is master of the situation (see also 11:1–6).

(A) In the three central passages (vv 17–21, 22–25, 26–31) Jesus is with the disciples, and is the major actor.

(see boxed texts left and right)
However, in verses 17 to 21 and verses 26 to 31 he predicts the future betrayals, denials, and flight *of the disciples*. All three scenes have Jesus at the centre of the action, and they form the central 'sandwich' (fifth, sixth and seventh in the middle of the eleven scenes) of 14:1–72. But in two of them (vv 17–21, 26–31), he shows his awareness of the oncoming darkness of the betrayal, the denials and the flight of those he had chosen and appointed to be with him in a special way (see 3:14). In the first of these three scenes, Jesus sits at the meal 'with the twelve' (vv 17–18), and predicts the horrible possibility that someone who shares his table fellowship will betray him. Amid consternation, and the dramatic repetition of 'Surely, not I?' as each person at the table asks that question (v 19), the breach of table fellowship by 'one of the twelve' is given as the sign (v 20). Yet, this terrible act is paradoxically part of God's design, in fulfilment of what was written of the Son of Man (v 21a). But there can be no exoneration of the betrayer (v 21bc).

(B) At the heart of 14:1–72 (the sixth of eleven scenes), dedicated to Jesus' never-failing presence to his disciples, Mark tells of Jesus sharing the intimacy of a meal with them. Jesus takes bread, breaks it and gives it *to the disciples* (v 22). He takes a cup, gives thanks and shares the wine *with the disciples* (v 23). The broken bread and the shared wine point forward to the events of the following day. Jesus tells *his failing disciples* that his broken body and spilt blood will set up a new covenant, recalling the words of Moses, as he ratified the original covenant with God: 'See the blood of the covenant that the Lord has made with you in accordance with all these words' (Ex 24:8). Mark's telling of his story of Jesus reaches one of its most poignant moments in a meal at which Jesus establishes a bond of loving self-gift with his disciples, who are about to betray, deny and abandon him.

Jesus sets up a new covenant through the sign of this broken

bread and shared wine, a sign of his gift of self *for others*, establishing a covenant of freedom and oneness with God: 'and all of them drank from it' (v 23b). The events of the following day will not bring this pact to an end. The word *until* rings out: 'I will never again drink of the fruit of the vine *until* that day (NRSV 'when') I drink it new in the Kingdom of God' (v 25). The readers must look beyond the coming death of Jesus. Mark has told this story of Jesus' final meal with his disciples to inform readers about his relationship with his disciples as well as his self-sacrifice in death. Mark's use of the story of the meal as the centrepiece of 14:1–72 allows him to highlight Jesus' unconditional response to the will of God in his unconditional gift of self for others (see 15:20b–25).

(A) The meal itself concludes with a hymn, but the focus of the narrative remains with Jesus and the disciples as, together, they move to the Mount of Olives (v 26). On arrival, Jesus again speaks to his disciples about the oncoming darkness and their failed discipleship. He, the shepherd, will be struck and they will all be scattered (v 27). However, in the midst of these threatening words, he makes a further prediction: 'But after I am raised up, I will go before you to Galilee' (v 28). They may flee in fear, but Jesus will go before them. Peter will not hear of failure. He swears unconditional adhesion to Jesus, however weak everyone else might be. But Peter is warned that before the cock crows twice, he will deny Jesus three times (vv 29–30). Peter swears allegiance unto death all the more vigorously (v 31a), and so do all the others: 'And all of them said the same' (v 31b).

(B) Jesus and the disciples gather in Gethsemane, as Jesus leaves them so that he might pray (v 32). He takes Peter, James and John with him, instructing them to watch with him, in his moment of anguish (vv 33–34). The storyteller gradually thins out the presence of the disciples as Jesus leaves the whole group, bringing only three of them with him. He prostrates himself before God in prayer, a prayer summed up in the words: 'Abba, Father, for you all things are possible; remove this cup from me; yet, not what I want, but what you want' (vv 35–36). Returning to Peter, James and John, he finds that they are not able to watch one hour with him, as they have fallen asleep (vv 27–38). Jesus is now totally alone. The irony of Jesus' command to his disciples 'to watch' in 13:33, 34,

Mark 14:17–31
(continued)

26 When they had sung the hymn, they went out to the Mount of Olives. 27 And Jesus said to them, "You will all become deserters; for it is written,

 'I will strike the shepherd, and the sheep will be scattered.

28 But after I am raised up, I will go before you to Galilee." 29 Peter said to him, "Even though all become deserters, I will not." 30 Jesus said to him, "Truly I tell you, this day, this very night, before the cock crows twice, you will deny me three times." 31 But he said vehemently, "Even though I must die with you, I will not deny you." And all of them said the same.

Mark 14:51–65

51 A certain young man was following him, wearing nothing but a linen cloth. They caught hold of him, 52 but he left the linen cloth and ran off naked.

53 They took Jesus to the high priest; and all the chief priests, the elders, and the scribes were assembled. 54 Peter had followed him at a distance, right into the courtyard of the high priest; and he was sitting with the guards, warming himself at the fire. 55 Now the chief priests and the whole council were looking for testimony against Jesus to put him to death; but they found none. 56 For many gave false testimony against him, and their testimony did not agree. 57 Some stood up and gave false testimony against him, saying, 58 "We heard him say, 'I will destroy this temple that is made with hands, and in three days I will build another, not made with hands.'"

(continued on page 37)

35 and 37 cuts deep, especially in the light of their recent vows of adhesion to Jesus, even if this means that they must die (14:29–31). Jesus returns to his prayer, repeating what he has already said and laying himself open to all that lies ahead (14:39). He revisits Peter, James and John, struggling against sleep and confusion (v 40). The passion is in motion: 'The hour has come; the Son of Man is betrayed into the hands of sinners. Get up, let us be going. See, my betrayer is at hand' (vv 41–42). The light of Jesus' unconditional self-gift to the will of the Father turns towards the darkness of betrayal.

(A) Judas, *one of the Twelve*, comes with weapons of violence and a crowd representing the Jewish leaders. Jesus' final words in Gethsemane (vv 41–42) lead directly to the following scene. He accepts the darkness that follows the light of his acceptance of the Father's will (vv 33–42). The hour has come (v 43). Now called 'the betrayer', Judas marks out Jesus with the title 'Rabbi', and a kiss, another breach of the intimacy established in 3:14 and in the shared meal (14:22–25). Jesus is taken by force (vv 44–46). Violence surrounds the moment, as someone standing by takes a sword and cuts off the ear of the high priest's servant. But Jesus reminds them of his presence among them, teaching in the Temple (see 11:11 – 13:37). Ironically, the suffering of the righteous one, long predicted in the Scriptures of Israel, must be fulfilled. The scene rushes to an end as Jesus' prophecy in 14:27 is fulfilled. The shepherd is struck; 'all of them deserted him and fled' (v 50). The storyteller provides a commentary on what has just happened by adding a tiny parabolic action. Another young man 'followed' Jesus, and his action comments upon the present situation of the disciples. Just as they fled in fear, so does this young man, but he leaves behind the linen cloth, his only article of clothing (vv 51–52). He, like the disciples who have fled, is naked in the nothingness generated by separation from Jesus.

(B) The accusation and condemnation is the moment for the formal proclamation of the truth about Jesus.

(see boxed texts left and right)

Jesus, the leaders of Israel, Peter and the guards assemble. Peter, who had followed Jesus 'at a distance', now draws ominously close to the guards. He is sitting with them, and the readers recall that Jesus has foretold that Peter will deny him (vv 53–54; see v 30).

The process begins with a series of false charges, but there is no agreement in the testimony brought against Jesus. At the centre of the passage, the high priest rises and asks directly: 'Are you the Messiah, the Son of the Blessed One' (v 61). The reader recognises the titles given to Jesus in 1:1: the Christ and the Son of God. For the first time in the narrative Jesus affirms his role in God's design. He accepts the charge as stated: 'I am' (v 62a), but adds another function that has been growing in importance across the narrative. The Son of Man who must suffer at the hands of his accusers will be the same one who will be seated at the right hand of God, and will come with the clouds of heaven (v 62b). The accused will become the final judge.

Jesus proclaims the truth. The storyteller's presentation of the person of Jesus is summed up in verse 62: Jesus is the Christ, the Son of God and the Son of Man. On these grounds, Jesus is condemned, but falsely. The high priest asks: 'Why do we still need witnesses?' (v 63). Jesus is condemned for blasphemy, but on the basis of his own witness. Jesus' physical suffering begins as some spit at him and strike him, crying out, 'Prophesy!' (v 65). Ironically, the reader has seen the prophecies of Jesus concerning both Judas' betrayal (see 14:17–21) and the disciples' flight (see 14:27) come true. He has just prophesied about the final coming of the Son of Man (v 62). In the light of the very next episode, there is deep irony in the insults of his opponents. What Jesus says will happen does happen! God will have the last word in and through the vindicated Son of Man who will return as judge (v 62).

(A) Enigmatically, part of God's design is the failure of the disciples. Thus, the last of Jesus' prophecies uttered at the meal (14:17–31; see vv 30–31) comes true. Peter, now 'with the guards' (v 54), denies any knowledge of the maid's suggestion that he was 'with Jesus, the man from Nazareth' (vv 66–68a). He moves closer to the gateway, but is trapped again as the maid makes more public that Peter was 'one of them', and again he denies this (vv 68b–70a). Now a matter of public discussion, one of the bystanders identifies Peter as a Galilean, and insists that he belonged to Jesus' followers. In his final denial, Peter rejects Jesus: 'I do not know this man you are talking about' (vv 70b–71). By the time the cock crows, Peter has denied Jesus three times. He broke down and wept (v 72). Although the disciples have dominated 14:1–72, playing an active role in the scenes marked (A), they will not appear again.

Mark 14:51–65
(continued)

59 But even on this point their testimony did not agree. 60 Then the high priest stood up before them and asked Jesus, "Have you no answer? What is it that they testify against you?" 61 But he was silent and did not answer. Again the high priest asked him, "Are you the Messiah, the Son of the Blessed One?" 62 Jesus said, "I am; and 'you will see the Son of Man seated at the right hand of the Power,' and 'coming with the clouds of heaven.' "

63 Then the high priest tore his clothes and said, "Why do we still need witnesses? 64 You have heard his blasphemy! What is your decision?" All of them condemned him as deserving death. 65 Some began to spit on him, to blindfold him, and to strike him, saying to him, "Prophesy!" The guards also took him over and beat him.

DID YOU KNOW?

• There are no stories of Jesus' birth and infancy in Mark's Gospel

• Mark tells the story of Jesus' last week in detail

• Mark depicts Jesus as suffering yet victorious

THE ROMAN TRIAL: CRUCIFIXION, DEATH AND BURIAL OF JESUS (15:1–47)

In 15:1 Jesus is led to Pilate. From here he will proceed to Golgotha (15:22) and to a grave (15:46). The steady movement from a focus upon Jesus (B) to a focus upon Romans and others continues over nine brief scenes (A). As 14:1–72 closed with the Peter scene (A), 15:1–47 opens with a scene with Jesus at its centre (B).

(B) The crowing cock indicates that it is morning. The action, described with care by Mark, links the Jewish and Roman trials. The leaders of the Jews and the Sanhedrin lead Jesus away and then hand him over to Pilate (15:1). The Roman Procurator asks a Roman question: 'Are you the King of the Jews' (v 2a), and as in 14:62, Jesus accepts this proclamation of the truth (v 2b). The chief priests continue to accuse Jesus (v 3), but Jesus remains silent. Pilate is amazed (v 5).

(A) Neither Jesus nor Barabbas are present. Barabbas was a revolutionary and murderer (vv 6–7). When the crowd asks that Pilate release a prisoner, as was his custom, Pilate ironically proclaims the truth. He presents Jesus as 'the King of the Jews' (v 9). But the leadership sways the people; and they ask for Barabbas (v 11). The storyteller has presented two absent characters to the reader: Barabbas the murderer and Jesus the King. The crowd chooses the murderer.

(B) Jesus is a suffering King. Pilate presents Jesus to the crowd as 'the King of the Jews', asking what they want done to him (v 14). Now both Jesus and Barabbas appear (v 15). The crowd demands that Jesus be crucified (vv 13, 14), despite Pilate's insistence that he is innocent (v 14). Mark reports Jesus being handed over to death, despite the clear evidence that he is an innocent King. Truth is rejected as the crowd twice demands that Jesus be crucified. Pilate gives in: 'So Pilate, wishing to satisfy the crowd, released Barabbas for them; and after flogging Jesus, he handed him over to be crucified' (v 15). Jesus' opponents choose a violent revolutionary instead of the innocent King of the Jews.

(A) Jesus is present, but entirely passive as the cohort of soldiers mockingly dress him as a King (vv 16–17). The storyteller has the soldiers ironically proclaim the truth: 'Hail, King of the Jews!' (v 18). They prostrate themselves fittingly, but they strike him and spit upon him. These actions indicate that, while they proclaim the truth, they reject what they are proclaiming (v 19). To make this clear, he is stripped of the purple cloak, a symbol of his royalty (v 20a).

(B) A number of features single out verses 20b to 25 as a self-standing unit.

(see boxed text left)

MARK 15:20B–25

Then they led him out to crucify him.

21 They compelled a passer-by, who was coming in from the country, to carry his cross; it was Simon of Cyrene, the father of Alexander and Rufus. 22 Then they brought Jesus to the place called Golgotha (which means the place of a skull). 23 And they offered him wine mixed with myrrh; but he did not take it. 24 And they crucified him, and divided his clothes among them, casting lots to decide what each should take.
25 It was nine o'clock in the morning when they crucified him.

There are nine brief scenes across 15:1–47. The crucifixion of Jesus forms the central fifth passage. The Romans continue to direct the action. As the passage opens we read: 'Then they lead him out *to crucify him*' (v 20b). It closes with the words: '*they crucified him*' (v 25b). The scenes before and after the crucifixion are full of violence and the screaming of abuse (vv 16–20a and vv 26–32). In the report of the crucifixion everything takes place in silence. There is no spoken word. Every verb in the passage has 'they' as the subject (meaning the soldiers), and tells of what the Romans do to Jesus: verse 20b: 'they led'; verse 21: 'they compelled'; verse 22: 'they brought'; verse 23: 'they offered'; verse 24: 'they crucified' and '[they] divided'; and verse 25: 'they crucified'. As Jesus is led out (v 20a), Simon of Cyrene, someone well known to the Markan community, takes up the cross and follows Jesus (v 21).

Roman procedure is followed as Jesus is crucified at Golgotha, but deeper themes are paramount. Jesus refuses anything that might lessen his unconditional response to the Father (v 23). The division of his garments recalls Psalm 22:18, and the reference to 'nine o'clock' (original: 'the third hour') begins to mark the time frame for Jesus' agony. The storyteller's use of this time frame (see v 33: 'noon' [original: 'at the sixth hour']; v 34: 'at three o'clock' [original: 'at the ninth hour']) shows how carefully God took care of the events surrounding the death of his Son. In a mysterious way, God's design is being worked out in this brutal murder. Mark 15:20b–25 describes Jesus' unconditional response to the will of God in his unconditional gift of self for others. This repeats the Eucharistic message of 14:20b–25, the centrepiece of 14:1–72.

(A) The kingship of Jesus is proclaimed in the title on the cross, 'The King of the Jews' (v 26), and then follows the information that two robbers were crucified on either side of Jesus (v 27).

(see boxed text right)
Two thieves have taken the positions of honour requested by the sons of Zebedee in 10:37, one on the left and one on the right of the crucified Christ. It closes with another proclamation, 'the Messiah, the King of Israel' (v 32a), and a remark from the storyteller that the two robbers joined in the abuse of Jesus (v 32b).

Between the frame of verses 26 to 27 and verse 32 (the proclamation of Jesus' dignity and the presence of the two thieves), passers-by recall the tradition of the construction of a new Temple

Mark 15:26–27, 29–32

26 The inscription of the charge against him read, "The King of the Jews." 27 And with him they crucified two bandits, one on his right and one on his left. 29 Those who passed by derided him, shaking their heads and saying, "Aha! You who would destroy the temple and build it in three days, 30 save yourself, and come down from the cross!" 31 In the same way the chief priests, along with the scribes, were also mocking him among themselves and saying, "He saved others; he cannot save himself. 32 Let the Messiah, the King of Israel, come down from the cross now, so that we may see and believe." Those who were crucified with him also taunted him.

of God (v 29). They demand that Jesus show his authority by *coming down from the cross* (v 30). We already know that Jesus is the cornerstone of the new Temple of God (see 12:10–11, 22–25), and that only by *remaining on the cross* will he found the new community of God. The Jewish leaders acknowledge Jesus' saving presence among others, but answer the request of the passers-by by telling them that he cannot save himself (v 31). They will only see and believe in Jesus' claim to be the Christ and the King of Israel (see 14:61–62a; 15:2) if he *comes down from the cross* (v 31a). But we know that only *on the cross*, abused and insulted, is Jesus Saviour, Christ and King of Israel. The crucifixion of the Messiah and Son of God, accompanied by the abuse of bystanders and Jewish leaders, is perhaps the most powerful piece of ironic writing in the Gospel of Mark.

(B) The words 'When it was noon' (15:33) introduce the report of the three hours that led to the death of Jesus 'At three o'clock' (15:34). Jesus is the focus of attention at all times, as he sinks into desolation, crying out in Aramaic, 'My God, my God, why have you forsaken me' (v 34). The use of Psalm 22, the lament of the righteous sufferer that has dominated the Markan passion story (see 14:17; 15:24, 29, 30–31), reaches its climax in these final words of Jesus in this cry. The sense of abandonment and the intensity of the question that Jesus asks in death must be maintained to capture the storyteller's presentation of the crucified Christ. The cry of 'My God' (in Hebrew/Aramaic: *eloi*) is misunderstood as a cry to Elijah, the helper of the helpless. The bystanders are still hoping that, at this last moment, Jesus will come down from this cross. His response is a further agonised scream, and he breathes his last (v 37). Only *after* his death, the Holy of Holies, once hidden from the world by a curtain, is revealed as the curtain is torn from top to bottom. The Temple is now available for the world to see. The centurion, who, facing Jesus, has witnessed Jesus' death, confesses: 'Truly this man was God's Son' (v 39). The death scene is the summit of Mark's narrative, the final resolution of the question behind the Gospel: who is Jesus?

(A) New characters appear in verses 40–41: Mary Magdalene; Mary the mother of James the younger, of Joses, and Salome (v 40b); and other unnamed women (v 41b). The three named women and the larger group have been associated with Jesus from his time in

Galilee. This links the women with the earlier teaching and ministry of Jesus, as they have followed and served him. The 'following' and the 'serving' must be given their full meaning: the women's past activities respond to Jesus' teaching on discipleship. But now, at the cross, they are described as 'looking on from a distance' (v 40). The disciples, and especially the Twelve, have abandoned, betrayed and denied Jesus. The women are still 'with Jesus' (see 3:14). But Mark's careful indication of their looking on from afar associates them with the vacillating Peter as Jesus began his passion. Peter also remained with Jesus after the arrest, but looked on 'from afar' (see 14:54).

(B) The body of Jesus is at the centre of this episode. The arrival of the evening of preparation for the Sabbath generates the need for Jesus' body to be hastily buried. He must not be left hanging on the cross until after the Sabbath (v 42). Joseph of Arimathea appears for the first time, a man of some influence. He has the courage to ask for the body, and, after checking with the centurion as to whether or not Jesus was already dead, Pilate grants the body to Joseph (vv 43–45). The body is hastily buried, without washing and anointing. Yet Joseph wraps the body in a freshly purchased linen shroud, mentioned twice in verse 46a, and lays the body in a tomb hewn out of the rock. A stone is rolled across the entrance to seal the tomb (v 46b). These details highlight Joseph's influence and care for the body of Jesus, but also prepare for the events that will take place 'after three days' (see 8:31; 9:31; 10:32–34).

Two of the women who stood at the cross, Mary Magdalene and Mary the mother of Joses (see v 40), see where Jesus was laid (v 47). This is not the end of the story. The timing of the episode points the reader to the day after the Sabbath (v 42; see 16:1). The body is not properly prepared for burial, and women who saw him die (vv 40–41) have also watched to see where he was hurriedly buried (v 47; see 16:1). Jesus is wrapped in a linen cloth, the covering used in the description of the young man who fled from Gethsemane, a parabolic comment upon the flight of the disciples (14:50). Mark has led us through the tale of the death of the Son of God and the burial of his dead body. We now wait for God's response to Jesus' question in 15:34: 'My God, my God, why have you forsaken me?'

DID YOU KNOW?

- Mark and the other evangelists were interested in conveying theological truths about Jesus rather than historical facts, although their narratives are based in authentic memories of the life and teaching of Jesus

- They wanted to express the good news about what God has done for us in and through Jesus Christ

The epilogue: Mark 16:1–8

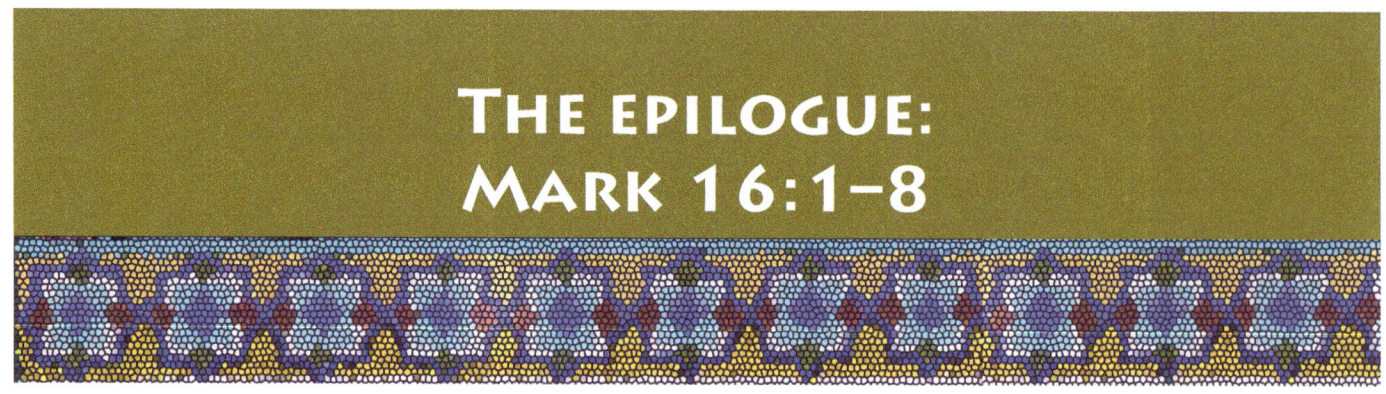

Mark 16:1–8

When the sabbath was over, Mary Magdalene, and Mary the mother of James, and Salome bought spices, so that they might go and anoint him. 2 And very early on the first day of the week, when the sun had risen, they went to the tomb. 3 They had been saying to one another, "Who will roll away the stone for us from the entrance to the tomb?" 4 When they looked up, they saw that the stone, which was very large, had already been rolled back. 5 As they entered the tomb, they saw a young man, dressed in a white robe, sitting on the right side; and they were alarmed. 6 But he said to them, "Do not be alarmed; you are looking for Jesus of Nazareth, who was crucified. He has been raised; he is not here. Look, there is the place they laid him. 7 But go, tell his disciples and Peter that he is going ahead of you to Galilee; there you will see him, just as he told you." 8 So they went out and fled from the tomb, for terror and amazement had seized them; and they said nothing to anyone, for they were afraid.

The setting of the first Easter morning is provided in verses 1 to 4. Links are made with the passion story: the Sabbath has now passed, and the women who were at the cross and at the tomb bring spices to anoint Jesus' body. Light is dawning on this 'first day of the week' as they approach the tomb, asking who will roll away the stone (vv 2–3)? Why anoint a dead body after three days? Why did they not think of the stone before they left home? Indeed, the stone was very large, but it had already been rolled back (v 4). The passive use of the verb in the sentence: the stone 'had already been rolled back' indicates that someone else has entered the story. Who might that be?

Answers come at the empty tomb (vv 5–7). As the women enter it, they see a young man sitting on the right side, dressed in a white robe (v 5). This description recalls the symbolic sign of the failing disciples: the young man who was dressed in a linen cloth and fled naked in his nothingness (see 14:51–52). Discipleship will be restored, despite fear and flight (see 14:50). The words of the young man in verse 6 tell them that they are looking in the wrong place. They are seeking Jesus, the Nazarene, the crucified. They are told to look at the place where the dead body had been laid. He is not there, because *he has been raised!* The answer to the question concerning the rolling back of the stone is answered: God has entered the story and has raised Jesus (v 6). Jesus' question from the cross, 'My God, my God, why have you forsaken me?' (15:34), has been answered. The Father has not forsaken the Son, in whom he is well pleased (see 1:11). The final words of the young man recall Jesus' promise of 14:28. The women are told to announce the Easter message: 'But go, tell his disciples and Peter that he is going ahead of you to Galilee; there you will see him, just as he told you' (v 7). In 14:28 Jesus promised that, despite the failure of the disciples, he *would go* before them to Galilee; in 16:7 the young man announces he *is going* before them into Galilee.

But the women run away from the tomb, associating themselves with the fear, trembling, astonishment and flight of the disciples (see 14:50–52). They say nothing to anyone, for they were afraid (v 8). Thus the Gospel of Mark comes to a close. Even the first readers of Mark knew of the tradition found in the other canonical Gospels: women were the recipients of the Easter message, and they delivered it to the disciples (see Mt 28:7–10; Lk 24:8–9; Jn 20:1–2). Mark the storyteller has *deliberately changed a well-known tradition*. He does this because he wishes to lead his readers back to the point where they began. In 1:1–13 the storyteller challenged readers by means of his Christological prologue. His main focus in 16:1–8 is again his readers, called to discipleship, meeting the risen Jesus in Galilee.

The epilogue makes clear that God's action is *not* the result of human initiative, but rests entirely with God. As with the promises of Jesus' forthcoming death and resurrection (8:31; 9:31; 10:33–34), the promises of 14:28 and 16:7 will be fulfilled. *What Jesus said would happen, will happen.* The challenges made by his enemies to prophesy (14:65), the failure of the disciples (14:50; see v 27), the betrayal of Judas (14:43–46; see 17–21), the denials of Peter (14:66–72; see vv 30–31), and Jesus' arrest, trials and crucifixion have all shown that Jesus' predictions come true. We have every reason to believe that the promises very existence *of the story* tells the reader that *what Jesus said would happen, did happen*. The faith-filled prologue of the Gospel tells of God's design for the human situation in the gift of his Son (1:1–13). The believing community is addressed in the epilogue (16:1–8). The disciples and Peter did see Jesus in Galilee, as he had promised (14:28; 16:7). Jesus' prophecies came true (see 8:31; 9:31; 10:32–34; 12:11–12; 14:17–21, 27–31). We accept that the promises of 14:28 and 16:7 also came true. There can be no record of any such encounter *within the narrative*. Jesus' words to his disciples on the Mount of Olives ring out: 'Heaven and earth will pass away, but my words will not pass away'

DID YOU KNOW?

• The resurrection is not directly described in any of the four Gospels

• The four evangelists looked back to the Jesus traditions they received and forward to the present and future needs of their own communities

• The Gospel narratives are theologically not historically motivated

• The Gospel of Mark was neglected by early Christian traditions and only found favour with scholars at the end of the eighteenth century

of 14:28 and 16:7 *have already come true*. The women do not obey the word of the young man. They, like the disciples, fail. As with the disciples, they flee in fear (16:8).

When and how does Jesus' meeting with the failed disciples, women and men alike, take place? The answer to that question cannot be found *in the story*; but the (13:31). For this reason, the voice from heaven tells all disciples, and readers of and listeners to the story of the Gospel of Mark: 'listen to him!' (9:7). If the promise of 14:28 and 16:7 had been thwarted, there would be no Christian community and no Gospel of Mark. We would not be reading this Gospel, much less this book today.

A Friendly Guide to Mark's Gospel 43

A Friendly Guide to the New Testament
Francis J Moloney SDB

Who wrote the New Testament? How has it come down to us in its present form? What did the life, death and resurrection of Jesus Christ mean for Jesus' first followers, St Paul and the early Christians? How can we use New Testament Scripture to deepen our faith? These questions are addressed in this guide which is written from historical and faith-based perspectives and is designed for those who are new to Bible study. It contains readings and commentary on specific passages of Scripture, icons, photos and original artwork, and a step-by-step guided experience of praying with Scripture.

A Friendly Guide to Jesus
Andrew Hamilton SJ

This book looks for answers to questions about Jesus. Not just who was he but who is he for us today. How can faith in Jesus help us to understand what really matters? What does it mean to be a follower of Jesus — how can we live happily and well as Christians? It is a guidebook in the search for meaning. Throughout this book Jan Hynes's stunning paintings of the urban landscape of contemporary Australia, as well as one of Australian wilderness, illustrate the life of Jesus in a fresh and vivid way.

A Friendly Guide to the Mass
Tony Doherty

For Catholics the celebration of the Mass is central to the expression of their faith. It is celebrated thousands of times a day in many places, in many languages, by many, many people and has been celebrated every day for centuries. It has many names and a variety of cultural guises. It means different things to different people. This guide opens up the treasures of the Mass and through story, humour, history and colourful imagery it offers us an insight into the heart of this ritual which is at once both ancient and new. There are references to the Catechism and the Scriptures, useful facts and reflective quotes.

A Friendly Guide to Prayer
Michael Whelan SM

'Listen with the ear of the heart.' This simple yet profound phrase from St Benedict is central to the message of this book which is a gentle guide and challenging coach, encouraging the reader to broaden and deepen their prayer life, offering support and providing opportunities for experience as well as knowledge. Each chapter contains sections 'For reflection' and 'For practice' to inspire readers to make the best use of the material presented. The book explores the rich, varied and complex tradition of prayer within the Catholic Church and urges the reader to slow down and listen to the text on the page and the text of their own heart.

Other titles include
John's Gospel
Luke's Gospel
Matthew's Gospel
Vatican II

www.ingramcontent.com/pod-product-compliance
Lightning Source LLC
Chambersburg PA
CBHW061100170426
43199CB00025B/2948